FIGHT
of my Life

KING BENJAMIN

This is a King Benjamin Presents publication
Fight of My Life: A Memoir
Copywrite © 2021 by King Benjamin.
This book is published under the copywrite laws of the United States. All rights reserved. No part of this book may be used, reproduced, stored, in a retrieval system, or transmitted, in any form or by any means, electronic, mechanical, photocopying, recording, or otherwise without expressed written consent from King Benjamin Presents except in the case of brief quotations embodied in critical articles and reviews.

Cover design: Michael Corvin
Editor: Likely Write Editing

DEDICATIONS

This book is dedicated to my daughter Dalejah and every single hood and ghetto across America and worldwide. Don't give up on your dreams! Rest in peace my brother Joe Black, Ty, Tommy T, Don, Wack, Stink, Big Pooh, TyKiese, and Lil' Tim.

ACKNOWLEDGMENTS

I would've never made it this far alone, so I want to thank everyone that has help me along the journey. First, I have to thank God for saving my life over and over. My biggest supporter in the world my mom, Alberta. My best friend and partner in crime Lakelia Deloach-Lucus aka (Author Blackbyrd), Duck, Duke, Kurtis, India Norfleet, Danielle Marcus, Destiny Horne, my sisters Melanie and Tisha, Mark Lenard, Mean Gene, and Nard. Last but certainly not least all my readers and supporters new and old. Thank you all for making this possible!

FOREWORD

I ALWAYS KNEW I WANTED the world to hear my story even before I had a story to tell. I never knew it would be so loaded with danger, messages, and testimony, but I knew it would be worth sharing. When I was a kid, I used to daydream of being a rap star and how I would blow up and they would make a movie about my life. In the hood, dreams are almost never realized but more often, destroyed and forgotten.

When I got older, I realized I didn't want to be a rapper. The big stage wasn't where I wanted to be. Whatever I decided to be, I'd have a long road to travel coming from where I was from. I don't wanna sound like I'm one of those people who used their circumstances as excuses, I'm just stating the facts. I didn't come from a long line of ambitious, hustling go-getters. Nothing I obtained in life was ever given to me by chance or luck. Maybe I won a few hundred at a dice game or the casino, but for the rest of it, I had to grind.

I always felt that anybody could write a book on their life filled with all the trials they've been through, but that doesn't mean people will want to read it. Everybody's been through stuff. I decided to tell my story for a few reasons. One is my obvious love for writing; two, I don't like talking about my life on social media platforms, it just seems weird for me. Lastly, I believed God had a big plan for me, and this is just the first phase. I've done a lot of wrong in my life, but with God's help, I was able to turn it around. I believe if my book gets into the right hands, it could be a catalyst for change for those that society has written off.

I think I got the first inspiration to write this book the way it was written after I read 50 Cent's autobiography years ago titled *From Pieces to Weight*, it's a must read. His book was not only entertaining, it was helpful and inspiring. Those are all the things I hope to accomplish with this book. I know the ghetto can seem like the darkest place in the world sometimes and just makes you wanna say "I quit!" If there's one message I'd like people to take away from my story, it's to never give up on yourself. Never throw in the towel. Here's my story.

HOW IT ALL STARTED

I WAS BORN IN THE MID-SEVENTIES to Alberta Jackson and Ronny Cheeks. My birth records have me as a Jr., even though I only carry my father's first name and none of his characteristics. To this day, his face is a vague image that depletes my energy whenever it surfaces on my mental screen. It's a good thing I don't have the same last name of a man I never really got to know. The only things I really know about my father is that he started out as a hustler and a gambler, but somewhere down the road, life took its toll like a turnpike and led him down a path of drug abuse and disappointment. I've only seen my biological father once that I can remember. He came to pick me up and spend the day with me when I was about twelve years old.

He called sometimes while living in New York, making promises he never would keep. The rumor around town was that he was in New York because he owed people money in Detroit and they were looking for him. When I got older, I remember thinking, this coward let niggas run him out of his own city? What a joke! When my mother was pregnant with me, she said some guys came into the house looking for him with guns. That was the last day of their relationship. She packed up and left the next day.

Being a big gambler, I figured out his hustle didn't outweigh his gambling addiction, which was why he probably stayed in the red. The only other thing I really knew about him was that he was a really good painter. I guess that's how he

KING BENJAMIN

survived once his hustle hand died out. When he finally came back to Detroit, he was basically a broken man. Just another drunken addict in the neighborhoods he roamed. I vowed to never let my enemies pressure me into fleeing my native land, even before I ever had enemies, because of seeing what had happened to his life. When I was around 16, he died in a house fire started by kerosene heaters. My artic cold bitterness wouldn't allow me to attend the funeral. I said fuck him to anybody that would listen because in my eyes, he'd been saying fuck me all my life.

Not having my father around really ate me up as a kid, but today it's a constant reminder of the importance of parenthood. Now, my mom was everything to me. She used to seem like the most overprotective person in the world, but she was always there for me and my older brother. She grew up in Mississippi and came from a pretty toxic environment herself. She suffered with bouts of depression and mental illness later in life that to this day she blames on her childhood. But growing up, she was the strong black mother trying her best to raise her kids the right way. My brother and I had different dads. Although the relationship didn't work out, unlike my dad, his father stuck around to raise him.

When I was about two years old, my mom married my stepdad. These would be the two male figures in my life from that point on. My stepdad was a good provider, but he didn't spend much time with us. On the weekends, he liked to drink and hang out with his friends. My brother's father had a good job, so he spoiled his son and looked out for me sometimes as well. We would go over to his house on the weekends and he would order pizza or take us to all the fun places to hang out. Every weekend, we were at the movies, go-cart racing, horseback riding, you name it.

It was a lot of fun, but it would always make me think where the hell is my daddy? As my brother Black—as most knew him by—got older, his clothes became more expensive

FIGHT OF MY LIFE

and that meant the less his father could do for me. At that point, it didn't matter because he had already shown me a ton of love and more importantly, what a real father was supposed to be like. I knew my stepdad loved us, but he wasn't good at expressing it. He was a military guy who had fought in the Vietnam War. I think his military life was the thing he was the most proud of because his face lit up when he told those stories.

I watched my mother and stepdad work their entire lives and not even sniff the scent of the American dream. I think it really affected the way I looked at the legit way of doing things. My mother never finished high school or learned to drive, so I'm sure she missed a lot of opportunities because of that, but more than anything was the systematic oppression of being born in Mississippi that led the way for all of her circumstances. We definitely had our ups and downs financially but as I got older, things only got worse.

For the first half of my childhood, I grew up in the area of Detroit known as the Black Bottom. It's supposed to be Detroit's first black neighborhood where people came when they migrated from the south. By the time I was born, it was grimy as hell. I remember I watched a guy get stabbed in the stomach right in front of our house. I was probably about eight years old and I remember he looked like he was in so much pain lying in the street, moaning loudly. It was a different kind of battle cry I would never forget. Then there was the time my stepdad shot a guy with his rifle and paralyzed him for life. We were all sitting on the porch on a summer night when this guy came up and asked him for a cigarette. When he refused, the guy grew angry and cocked back and punched him before taking off running. My pops gave chase, but this dude was crack-head fast.

Pops came back to the house steaming mad. He paced to the front porch with deadly intentions, inhaling the very vice that sparked the altercation. About thirty minutes later, the dude appeared on the corner of the block next to the

KING BENJAMIN

barbershop like nothing had happened. He had his back turned, talking to some other guys.

"I'm not chasing this nigga again. Bert, where's my gun?" I heard him say as he stormed into the house.

My mom made us go in the house while she tried to talk him down, but Pops wasn't having it. He emerged from the bedroom with a rifle with a scope on it. He walked out onto the porch with the rifle and seconds later, we heard the terrifying shots ring out. Blah, Blah, Blah! I remember me and my brother sitting in the bedroom straight shook. Nothing like that had ever happened at our house. In the following days, I would hear Pops tell his friends about it.

He told them his target went down on the first shot. The second and third shot was just to scare off his friends. I don't remember what happened after that, but nobody snitched, and the next time I saw the dude who asked for a cigarette, he was in a wheelchair. Thinking back on it now, it's crazy how one stupid decision can change a person's life forever. Luckily, that person wasn't my dad.

We lived in a two-family house at the time and the people that lived upstairs were just downright trifling. They had roaches, mice, and all kinda unidentifiable shit running around up there. You might fuck around and run into a skunk or a racoon inside the enclosed back porch that led to upstairs. When we opened the back door, all you could smell was funk and mildew from piles of clothes stored on the back porch and everywhere they could find to put them. They had a water leak that eventually made our living room ceiling collapse, and that was the last straw, thank God.

We started looking for a new place, and it turned out my pops' brother was moving from his house and wanted to rent it out. The house was on Van Dyke and McNichols (Six Mile). His house was a three-bedroom, brick, ranch-style home, and it was much nicer than the one we lived in so it wasn't a hard

FIGHT OF MY LIFE

decision to make. We bounced and I never had to deal with roaches again. But this new neighborhood was where everything that shaped and molded me into the man I am today started.

WELCOME TO VAN DYKE

VAN DYKE WAS A LOT LIKE The Bottom as far as the poverty and the number of cutthroats and savages roaming around the hood. But it was the mid-80s and crack was still very new, so it hadn't destroyed the neighborhood just yet. For the most part, it was a functioning community. There weren't a lot of vacant houses or abandoned buildings. It was actually a nice-looking area back then, but the streets were slowly taking it over.

At this time, I was an angel in my mom's eyes. I was brighter than the average student, always on the honor roll, and even won a few spelling bee contests. I got a chance to compete on a larger scale against schools from all over the city, but I think my nervousness got the best of me then. Math was a subject that didn't come easy for me, but there was nothing I couldn't grasp when I put my mind to it. My brother Black was the troubled child and his grades were never satisfactory for my parents.

Once I reached middle school, I started to think less about school and more about girls. Mesmerized by beauty and early development, my head came out of the books and floated up onto a cloud where it would stay the next couple of years. My best friend at the time was named Bill. He thought we were so cool that he felt it was okay that he called me the first time he was able to jack off and actually bust a nut. He was so excited and happy, and I remember just thinking it wasn't something I wanted to hear about. It was funny the way he told

FIGHT OF MY LIFE

the story, but it was also fruity as hell. But Bill wasn't gay, we talked about girls all day every day. I wasn't that big on sports, but I loved swimming and gym because I got to see some skin. I played all the sports, football, basketball, and baseball; I just didn't excel at any of them. I was, however, a really good swimmer, so I just took pride in that.

Bill and I used to always argue about the silliest shit. Just boys being boys as we found our macho and competitive nature. He thought he knew it all, so sometimes I'd have to set him straight and prove he didn't. I don't remember what our biggest argument was about, but somehow it led to fist throwing in the middle of the classroom. All I remember was me getting up in his face provoking and pushing him as hard as I could. I wanted to fight so bad because I was angry and sick of Bill's shit. But keep in mind, I'd never actually had a fight before. I went through elementary school unscathed, mostly because of my older brother and my best friend Rock. But nobody was here with me, so I had to stand up for myself, which I didn't mind at all.

I pushed Bill one too many times and I could see the look in his eyes when he turned into the Incredible Hulk. Bill beat the breaks off me in front of the whole classroom. Needless to say, my first fight didn't go the way I planned it. Bill was much stronger than I thought, and he was able to overpower me and get off quick combos before I had time to recover. I don't remember who broke it up, but it was good thing they did. I needed more training in hand-to-hand combat if I was gonna be popping shit. I remember feeling so embarrassed that all the girls had seen me take an L like that. But it would be over twenty years later before I took another one.

****

Bill and I were back friends again in less than three months. It seemed like after a month or so, everyone had forgotten all about the fight, except for us. I don't think either of our lives were the same without that one homey you could trust with all your secrets. Besides that, we worked better together when it came to the ladies. We figured out that girls liked a guy with a sense of humor. With him being short and fat and me being dark and skinny with a wide nose, we needed to find some type of edge, so we became class clowns for a while just to get the girls' attention. We would always think of a way to make a scene and get the whole class involved. Wait for the teacher to turn her back and stomp on the floor as loud as we could. Soon as she turned around, everyone would stop on a dime. Still makes me laugh to this day thinking about how much hell we put the math teacher through.

Soon, she started riding us for every little thing, knowing we were behind most of the trouble. That just made it worse because there were more troublemakers that were just joining the team that were just downright evil. People started spitting in her coffee and things like that. I didn't go that far, but I would break pencils in the door so we would be locked out of the class when we came from lunch. She didn't deserve all we did to her but in my defense, my math teacher never liked me from day one. My brother Black had already put her through hell when he had her math class two years earlier. Seeing me walking into her classroom was like spotting a mouse running across the kitchen floor a week after the exterminator had been paid. So even though there were actually three or four people responsible for all the mayhem, I got the majority of the blame. I was getting the attention I wanted from girls, but my grades were plummeting. I went from a straight A student to C student to C and D student.

One day, the class went on a trip to the Science Center and to the Imax Theater. By this time, I was definitely one of the most popular guys in my class and my little circle of friends was a big deal. All the girls wanted to sit with us. I had the two girls that I knew I could feel up sit on opposite sides of me. They were both thick, but one had a big butt and small breasts, and the other had D-cup breasts in the seventh grade. When

FIGHT OF MY LIFE

the lights went out, I turned to CeCe with the D cups and slid my hand in her shirt. I used my free hand to unbutton her shirt until I could pull her nipple out. Once I had her breast out, I buried my face in her chest and had the time of my young life while they watched the movie.

My crew was getting busy as well, I found out later. We would talk about that whole experience for weeks to come. After that, having sex became a bigger focus and all I thought about most days. But as much fun and foreplay as I had, I still went to the eighth grade a virgin. Every girl I was in contact with after school lived way on the other side of town, and the girls in school just wanted to kiss. I started to focused on meeting new girls at school that might wanna go all the way.

NOT MOM'S PROUDEST MOMENT

AT THE HEIGHT OF MY POPULARITY, I met a girl named Christie. She was short, brown, and beautiful. I'd known her by face for a while, but I finally decided to step to her one day in the halls. She gave me her number and I quickly pursued. We hit it off, talking after school most of the time. Christie and I would stay up on the phone all times of night until the wee hours of the morning. I remember her parents worked the night shift and mine just slept hard, so it worked out. I don't know to this day that we were actually a couple, but in my eyes, we definitely were. I do remember that when we started talking, Christie was talking to another guy named Brelly. Both of us really liked her, so that caused a lot of tension between Brelly and me that would last for years to come.

Since she stayed up with me all night every night talking on the phone, I assumed she'd made her choice. I didn't have a phone in my room, so I had to wait until everyone was sound asleep and sneak in the den to call her. One night, about three in the morning, I was laid back engulfed in a deep conversation and falling deeper for Christie, when the light flicked on in the room. I froze like she'd pulled a gun on me as I spotted my mom standing in the doorway, eyes full of fury.

"Getcho ass off that phone!" she yelled.

FIGHT OF MY LIFE

"I—I gotta call you back," I mumbled before hanging up in Christie's face.

Mom scolding me for old and new, but all I could think about was did my girl hear me getting checked before I hung up the phone. I promised my mom I wouldn't do it again, but it would take armed security to keep me from making my late-night calls. I just couldn't stay away knowing that Christie would be up all night probably waiting for me to call. I figured if I didn't call, she would probably ended up talking to Brelly instead. A couple weeks later, I was back in the exact same spot lying on the floor with door closed, in the dark getting it in. I had Christy right where I wanted her. It was just a matter of time before I had her skipping school to come get naked for me, I thought.

All of a sudden, the light came on and the danger warning went off in my head. As soon as I looked up, there was a big black belt coming down on my ass. I quickly tried to hang up the phone before the beating started. I begged and pleaded, promising not to do it again, but that didn't stop my mom from tearing my ass up good. It was one of the worst ass whoopings I can remember receiving as a kid.

After that, I couldn't risk it anymore. Talking to Christie all night was dangerous. After some time, things started to fizzle out and I ended up kicking it with another girl that didn't want to do anything but kiss and hug. I decided to focus on my grades so I wouldn't end up repeating the eighth grade. By now, Bill and I had inducted another main man into our crew. The duo was now a trio. Hoolie, Bill, and I were inseparable in the eighth grade. We skipped school at Hoolie's house, trying to freak on girls, listening to New Edition's "Can You Stand The Rain." We also didn't allow anybody fucking with one of us without catching hell from all of us.

One day, Bill had an issue with Brelly, who was twice his size. The two of them started fighting in the gym. I saw Bill needed my help and I didn't hesitate. I ran from the bleachers

KING BENJAMIN

and got off five or six punches before Brelly grabbed a hold of me. Once he grabbed me, Bill was able got get off a quick combo. I shook loose from his grasp before he could throw a punch and by that time, the gym teacher and others ran in to break it up. Neither of us could beat Brelly one on one but together, he didn't stand a chance. But Brelly lived right near my house, only a few blocks over. I was hoping I didn't have to finish it later when I didn't have back up but if I did, so be it.

A couple months later, I had issues with a guy named Sam. I don't know why he never liked me, but I was cool with his brother. We had agreed to fight outside at three o'clock when school let out. I was ready. By now, I'd had enough brawls that I was confident in my hands. He showed up on time and so did I. The whole school was right there watching, so I didn't hesitate to set it off. I punched him in his shit and he stumbled. I rushed in for a combination, pinning him up against the gate. I had him right where I wanted him. I didn't need help, but I got some anyway.

I looked up and Hoolie and Bill were right there throwing punches. From that moment on, Sam didn't stand a chance. All of a sudden, I felt myself being yanked off of Sam and dragged across the schoolyard. I didn't realize it was the police until I was halfway to the squad car. And this was when I would get my first taste of police brutality. Without a word of provocation and zero resistance, I was punched in the side of the face twice by this angry white man with sandy brown hair.

I was a little dizzy and full of adrenaline as he tossed me in the back of the squad car with handcuffs on. Moments later, Sam was joining me. I don't know how or why it was only us that were taken to jail, but the craziest part of it all was that they took us to what was known as the gang unit, all the way on the westside off McGraw. Once we were taken inside and processed, I realized the faces in the cell behind me were familiar. It was my brother and his friend from the

FIGHT OF MY LIFE

neighborhood, Don. I couldn't believe we had both been arrested on the same day at different schools. I knew this wasn't going to be my mom's proudest moment.

KETTERING HIGH SCHOOL (KE)

AFTER THE EIGHTH GRADE, Bill and I stopped hanging. I think his pops got on him about playing around in school, and he started to clean up his act. We went to the same high schools but we just drifted apart. By now, I had a lot of homies, but Boogie and Sal were my main partners. All of us were alike in the sense that nobody was soft, but none of us was extremely aggressive. As we got older, we started hanging with older guys that were a lot more aggressive. A lot of them were my brother's friends, and they were already petty criminals. Some worked for big drug dealers and some sold dummy rocks to keep some cash.

They stole a lot too. Walked in the store and stuffed 40 ounces in their coats and walked out. My brother was into drugs by now as well. He'd get a sack from a dealer and go on Wisner Street and sell it in a couple hours. He spent most of the money getting drunk with his friends. At that age it wasn't much else he could do with the money without my parents getting suspicious.

My mom didn't approve of his friends so she watched him like a hawk, but once she went off to work, he was free to move how he felt. I remember one day, she caught him on the corner turning up a 40 ounce. She smacked fire out his ass when he got home, and he learned to be more discreet after that. In the 80s, they had gangs like Best Friends, HBOs, and 20/20, but in the 90s we just represented our hoods. We ran in packs like a gang but we never wanted to be looked at as one. Everybody

FIGHT OF MY LIFE

I ran with could handle their own without help, and we represented Van Dyke like a badge of honor.

I started Kettering High in fall of 1989 and it was a wild ride from the very start. I'm sure it was a challenge for most of us to learn anything in that environment. It had to be about ten different hoods or gangs that collided and would fight daily. Lucky for me, I was rolling with a crew of thoroughbreds. I was still running with Boogie and Sal but we looked up to my brother and his friends, so we'd find them and hang with them all day. When everybody linked up, we'd be about twenty-five deep, but only about fifteen of us actually belonged in the school. The rest had been banned from the school long ago but they still snuck in whenever they wanted.

I'd earned my respect from fighting in middle school, and now I felt like I could beat anybody my size and even bigger. One day I had to square up with a dude in KE that was the exact same size as me. It was a fight that started over nothing more than hard stares. Each time we saw each other, the staring match ensued. I think he ran with dudes my older friends didn't like. All I knew was after a few times, I said something. He replied and we argued briefly, but hall security broke it up. The next time I saw him, it was on.

We scrapped it out a good five minutes, each of us landing solid hits. He was fast, but so was I. As the crowd gathered, I could feel everybody was watching so I hit him with everything I had before security rushed us to the ground to break it up. At that point, I still felt like the fight was a draw. To tip the scales in my favor, I broke loose, ran up, and kicked him in the face while security still had him on the ground. The oohs and ahhs made me feel much better about claiming my victory, even if he was defenseless.

After that, dudes in my classes knew I would scrap in a minute. The older guys believe in me too. I was called on as the little enforcer a few times when guys my age would screw up the dope money they owed the older guys and couldn't pay.

KING BENJAMIN

As I beat up guys almost twice my size, it would increase my confidence that I could handle myself when the time came. I felt right at home at Kettering, even though it was complete chaos. Most of my friends drove stolen cars to school, but soon they stopped stealing them and started carjacking. We always had a way to school but we never stayed long. We'd hit the Sandwich Shop down the street for breakfast and then go to the store and get beer.

Back then, all the school doors were unlocked all the time, so anybody could come and go as they pleased. After drinking and smoking a couple blunts, then we were ready for class. We'd go back into the school but we usually just ended up flirting with girls until we got into a fight. Every day was filled with a different adventure, and I totally lost track of focusing on school or my future.

I can admit this was the one time in my life that I was being a follower, but back then, I certainly didn't feel like it. By now, my brother had been expelled from Kettering so whenever he came to the school, he was usually looking for trouble. My neighborhood was Van Dyke and Six Mile but Van Dyke runs very long, all the way from Eight Mile to Jefferson in Detroit alone. The railroad tracks were what divided the two neighborhoods that took up about sixty-five percent of Kettering students. It also divided us growing up as teenagers.

My brother and his friends always had enemies from the other side of the tracks because that's just the way things were. On this particular day, I didn't even know my brother was in the building until I saw him arguing with some dudes from the other side of the tracks. Boogie and I went and stood behind my brother so that people would know he wasn't alone. Security came and broke things up before it got out of hand, but it was far from over. When we left the scene, my brother was heated. I had information I knew he needed to hear.

FIGHT OF MY LIFE

"You know the whole crew is here today?" I said, meaning all the other troublemakers that didn't belong in the school, like him.

"Where?" he asked, eyes widening.

"I just left them around the corner," I said.

We took off in the direction I knew everybody was hanging out. We knew if we ran into the dudes he was arguing with and security wasn't around, they wouldn't hesitate to bomb first. Minutes later, we ran right into the whole V6 crew, as we liked to call ourselves back then. We explained what had happened and took off looking for the dudes we had beef with. By now, school was letting out so everybody was about to leave. It didn't take long for us to run right into the dudes we were looking for, but now we had them extremely outnumbered.

The biggest dude in our crew, Fats, grabbed the first nigga he saw and slung him right into a fiberglass window. Some of the niggas I was with pulled out miniature Louisville Sluggers like magic wands and started beating niggas in the head with them. I was running around just punching and kicking niggas that dropped to the floor, 'cause they really didn't need my help, but I was there. After beating the shit out of these guys for a couple minutes, I heard someone yell.

"Let's go! Let's go!"

We all took off running for the back doors. When we got outside, we were all excited and on an adrenaline high, just going over what had happened. As we reached the front of the school, we were all so excited we didn't even see there was someone standing on school grounds with a Tech Nine pointed right at us.

"Ahhhhh!" girls screamed and ran everywhere, taking cover.

We all took off running for our lives. Running through an open field, I realized I was an easy target, so I dropped down

KING BENJAMIN

and laid flat in the grass, but I still hadn't heard any shots. I rolled over and I saw that the guy's clip had fallen out of the gun, and he was fumbling with the clip trying to get it back in as the chaos continued. I think his gun had jammed while he was trying to shoot, which led to him adjusting the chamber and the clip falling out.

While he was doing all of that, I took the opportunity to jump up and dash back into the building. I don't remember what happened next, but he never got off a shot and we all met up on the block later on to have a good laugh about it. When I got home later that day, the police were everywhere but especially on my block. In the back of our house, the alley was taped off like it was a crime scene. The police were in the alley pulling out garbage bag after garbage bag. There were all kinds of unmarked cars and vans everywhere.

I was so anxious to find out what had happened. It didn't take long when my mom came from the neighbor's house and informed me. The police had found a head and body dismembered right in the garbage dumpster behind our house. The next day, we found out that it was a lady that used to babysit me and my brother when we lived in Black Bottom. All we ever found out about the incident was that it was drug related.

SELF-ESTEEM ISSUES

IT WAS A LOT FUN getting into so much trouble in high school, but I wasn't exactly happy deep down inside. I'd gone from being very popular in middle school to basically a gnat on the window ledge in high school. I wasn't super fresh and I wasn't bummy. I was average as hell, which didn't get me noticed by any of the girls I was interested in. I was already smoking weed because everybody I hung with was smoking. Weed altered my mind state and I became shy, withdrawn, and unsure of myself. Peer pressure at its finest. All of a sudden, it was hard for me to meet girls, and the only ones I really communicated with were the ones I knew from middle school.

One day, I met KeKe walking up the street. She was shaped like a grown woman, caramel brown, and had big, pretty eyes. She was just what I needed at the time, and I knew she wanted me just as badly when she started calling me all day every day. I had my mind on one thing and one thing only. Getting the virgin tag off my back.

About a week went by and I set up a date for her to come by my house while my parents were at work. She knew exactly what the date was all about. So after some small talk, we went upstairs to my bedroom and I made my move. I was nervous at first, and I had problems with the bra, but eventually, I got her naked. The whole thing probably lasted five minutes. My body was in shock, but my mind was at ease. I felt validated. I was no longer a virgin. I remember us sitting on the steps that led to my room upstairs while she tied her sneakers.

KING BENJAMIN

"You happy now you got some pussy, huh?" Keke said, smiling.

I just smiled too. I really was happy. After that, I think KeKe fell even harder for me, because she started blowing me up even more. I was ready to experience the next girls' bodies and didn't want a relationship yet. I knew KeKe would tie up too much of my time, so I started to distance myself. I answered less of her calls and got off the phone quickly when we did talk until she got the message. We would still talk here and there as friends, but we never had sex again. Looking back on it, I'd fucked up because I would continue to catch hell trying to get a girl at my school freshman year. I should've never let KeKe go.

I tried approaching some of the new chicks that I liked but I wasn't getting anywhere. The weed had my game nonexistent. I tried to talk to some of the girls from middle school that used to like me, but they all had boyfriends now. It wasn't long before I began to feel this anger inside that I couldn't explain, and I began to have fights for no reason. The crew I ran with outside of my two closest friends were older and popping. All the girls liked them because they stayed kicking up dust, and I was right there with 'em. But no matter how many fights I had, it still didn't seem to help anybody notice me. It just seemed like I went to school every day and became invisible. Then my self-esteem became so low I didn't want any attention from anyone. Now I just wanted a girlfriend. Not just somebody to have sex with, but somebody that I would still want to be around after the sex part.

Since I'd just about completely gave up on meeting a girl at school, I ended up meeting a girl over the phone through my cousin. This would become my first real girlfriend, Lisa. Lisa had a sexy voice and my cousin assured me she was pretty. I felt a connection to her almost immediately. My confidence wasn't an issue talking to a girl over the phone that I'd never met. From the first conversation, the vibe was different than

FIGHT OF MY LIFE

any girl I'd ever talked to. I reeled her in, giving her my whole bad boy history, and I guess she loved that about me so we agreed to meet. When we met face to face, the connection grew even stronger. I loved the way she smelled. I loved her eyes and her smile, but I kept all of this to myself. I knew she had other male friends.

I didn't have anybody around at the time, so I was really ready to give Lisa all of my attention. Just having her around changed my perspective almost immediately. I would break out my best gear every time I went to see her. Since we only saw each other on the weekend, it appeared that I was always fresh. I had come to realize that my school was a fashion show and if I wanted to be anybody in that place, I needed to get my ass on the runway. This was around the time my crew started robbing niggas for shoes, coats, jewelry, and whatever else they could find of value.

They would just ride up to a different high school every Friday, hop out, and start robbing niggas. I personally never put in any work at high schools but I would still reap the benefits, being the smallest one in the click. Whatever they couldn't fit was mine, so I had a lot nice shit I had to hide from my mom growing up. Being fly and consistent helped me bump out the rest of the dudes fighting for a position in Lisa's life, and we became a couple.

She went to Murry Wright and lived far away so even as couple, I still only saw her once or twice a week. That left me with a lot of time and eventually, I started to mess with other girls. I was just starting to heat up and make a name for myself in my sophomore year in high school when I was caught smoking weed in the hallway and expelled permanently. I had already been given three or four chances by the principal to straighten up my act. I'd been kicked out for all kinds of stuff and the smoking in the halls was the last straw.

My mom was so disappointed in me. By this time, my brother was in jail for a shooting inside a clothing store. Back

KING BENJAMIN

in '89, less than six months into my freshman year, my brother Black and a few friends were inside looking around when some big burly guys came in the store, purposely bumping into guys and stepping on shoes and being all kinds of disrespectful. A scuffle broke out and someone slid my brother a pistol. He opened fire right inside the store and shot all three of them. Luckily for him, he aimed below the waist. Each one of them got shot in the balls or the legs, and he fled the scene with the gun still in his hands. The state of shock must've made him run all the way to his friend's house like that, because witnesses reported seeing him running up Harper with the gun out for the world to see.

We he went to court, Black got lucky again by going in front of one of the most lenient judges on the bench at the time. He could see that the situation was truly self-defense and sentenced him to eighteen months up north. While bro did his time up at MTU, I got enrolled in Osborn High. This school was full of the prettiest girls on the east side and young drug dealers, which made it an even bigger fashion show. I was a nobody all over again, but I no longer cared about that.

I'd promised my mom that I would get back on course, so I was focused on that. I knew with Black in jail, I couldn't keep breaking her heart like I was. I concentrated on school and tried to get my grades back up. I had a one to eight schedule and I didn't skip any classes, even though we lived in walking distance from my school now. But with so many beautiful girls, school really was the best place to be, so that gave me extra incentive. I used to have the prettiest girls help me with my math, and then we would kick it after school.

I still had a girlfriend, but we weren't seeing each other as much as I would've liked. At this point, I could have probably went on a straight path and had a totally different life. Call it Karma or whatever, but I think the next few months changed my life forever.

TAKE THE PAIN AWAY

THINGS WERE REALLY GOING SMOOTHLY at school and my grades were starting to really pick up. I was at the point where I was carrying books to and from school again and doing all my homework. I'd made a few friends, but they were all focused on school too, so we just usually kicked it in class. One day, I was coming out of the school minding my business and got hit in the head with some sort of hard object. It didn't hurt, but it obvious to me someone had thrown it at me. I turned around fuming, and I saw a group of guys laughing and pointing at one guy in particular. His name was James and I knew this because as they pointed they were saying, "James did it, James did it!"

"You don't know me, nigga, to be playing with me," I challenged him through clenched teeth.

"What?" he replied with a scowl.

He'd already sized me up and decided I wasn't a threat.

"You heard me, nigga. You think I'm bitch or something?" I responded, ready for whatever happened next.

This was the kind of thing me and my friends did all the time back in KE. Pick on whoever, whenever we felt like it. But here I was, all alone and on the receiving end of it now. I had called him out in front of his friends, and now he was stepping to me removing his jacket, prepared to scrap. He was probably four inches taller and at least twenty pounds heavier than me, but that didn't concern me. I sat my books down near the steps. As soon as he was in reaching distance, I swung and connected. As we exchanged blows, I was only focused on James. I never saw anyone else approach me as we locked horns, but all of a sudden, I felt a flurry of punches, eight to ten fists pounding on me at once.

I knew James only had two fists, so this fight had quickly become extremely uneven and impossible to win. I tried my best to hold my ground, but I knew as the fists kept flying, I'd eventually get taken down. I wasn't about to get stomped out in front of the whole school, so I did the only logical thing to do. I had to turn and run for the first time in my life. I ran so fast and hard it took me a while to realize nobody was even chasing me. At that point, I could've stopped, but I kept running out of anger. The quicker I got home, the quicker I could get on the phone and call up my crew because in my young mind, somebody had to die for this.

This was a defining moment for me. This was when I knew that my anger could be used to bring out the worst side of me. I would later draw from the experience when creating the turning point for my character Chris aka Capone in my first novel, *Cry Baby*. My anger was on one thousand, but I remember thinking to myself that the guys that jumped me were soft. I left the fight on my feet and basically without a scratch. When my crew put in work, we left people seriously injured, but I wasn't even bleeding except for a small cut inside my mouth nobody could see. When I got home, I went straight to the phone. My plan was to find out who these punks were and kill 'em all. My rage had spiraled out of control. But by the time I got in touch with everybody I knew, the school would be empty so we waited. The next day, we rode up to Osborn around the same time school was letting out with two car loads full of niggas with big guns and plenty of ammo. It wasn't even about fighting anymore, it was about sending a message. You couldn't fuck with one of us. My anger hadn't subsided any overnight.

FIGHT OF MY LIFE

We pulled up right out in front of the school and hopped out. If you were there to see the looks on our faces, you knew what we came to do. I had my hand in my coat, walking around looking for James, ready to pull out and catch a life sentence without parole, and nobody was trying to stop me. I started asking people had they seen him and nobody dared tell me they had. I asked were any of his friends at school, but nobody wanted to get involved.

"When you see that bitch, tell him I got a bullet with his name on it," I threatened as I left, headed back to the car.

We came back for the next two days, but James was nowhere to be found. I knew he and his crew had to be hiding out now because a crew that big was never that hard to find. My guess was he played it smart the first day and then heard about the carload of niggas that came looking for him. From that day on, the crew that I was looking for dropped out of school as far as I know. I'd found out the names of some more of them, but they never came back. I went to plan B. I kept asking questions until I found out where James lived.

One morning, I stole my pops' car and drove to the house I knew James lived in on a solo mission. Pulled up out front and emptied a whole clip in the picture window out front. I still thank God to this day that I didn't hit anybody, but back then, I remember thinking the message had been sent and I felt a small piece of justice was done. Looking back on it now, I realized I shouldn't have involved his family, but I was young and dumb. I couldn't care less about innocent lives back then. This was the beginning of the devil finding a temporary home in my young, lost mind as he continued to harden my heart.

My pride was still bruised from being jumped but after that, I went back to school and held my head high. James wasn't there and I knew he wasn't coming back, and I knew I was the reason why. I tried to get back on track with my classes and once again, things were going smooth for a minute. Then they started doing these annoying hall sweeps every day. They literally only gave you time to walk from one class to another.

I would stop and talk to girls and stuff, so I always got caught up in hall sweeps. I wasn't moving any slower than anybody else, but I felt like this was high school not the military. I never liked discipline and it started to feel like they really wanted us to jog to class or some shit. In my mind, I'd come a long way and they should just be glad I was showing up and working hard in each class. Every day the bell would ring and then I'd hear,

"Hey you! Come here, where's your ID?"

On this particular day, I'd already been caught in one hall sweep. So when I was caught in the second one, I just said forget it, I'm going home. As I tried to leave, the head of security, who was also a police sergeant, told me I couldn't leave the school.

"I don't care what you say, I'm leaving," I replied.

He ran up on me like a tough guy and collared me up. He shoved me in the small closed foyer that led to a lower level. I wasn't expecting all of this just because I wanted to leave school.

"You think you tough?" he barked, still holding on to me.

He was snarling at me like a Pitbull. I went into fight or flight mode. I knew this was an invitation to fight, so I just hit him. I punched him right in the mouth with all I had, and he pushed me down about five steps to the lower level. I stumbled backwards into more security guards. I tried to gain my footing as they tackled me to the ground and handcuffed me. They pulled me up and sat me down in a steel chair. Once I was in the chair with my hands behind my back, the police sergeant took the opportunity to slap the living shit out of me.

"You bitch!" he screamed.

FIGHT OF MY LIFE

I was so mad a tear streamed down my face. Not because he'd slapped me, but because he did it when I was handcuffed and defenseless. I still couldn't believe all of this was happening just because I'd threatened to leave the school. I hadn't threatened him, and I hadn't initiated any physical altercation. Although I was only fifteen or sixteen at the time, I felt like a man. And I was told you never slap a man. Instead of going home, I went to jail as if I had assaulted him, even though he assaulted me first. And what made this whole situation way worse was when I got out, I told my mom exactly what happened and she didn't believe my story. I explained to her that I never threaten the cop or touched him. I never did anything that would've justified his behavior. When she took me back to school, he really threw on the charm and she continued to take his side. That was the moment I stopped caring about school.

I said fuck school, fuck trying to make people proud, fuck everything and everybody. I tried to do the right thing and it led to me getting slapped around and jumped on by the police. My self-esteem plummeted again. I felt like a real piece of shit that nobody really cared about. I was even mad at God because I'd felt like he sold me a dream about turning my life around. They say misery loves company and hurt people hurt people. During this time, I wanted the world to suffer with me. For the next few weeks, I contemplated killing the officer that slapped me. I figured I could catch him in the parking lot going home and put a couple bullets in his head then once he was down, I'd follow through with a couple more shots.

I knew he carried a 357 Magnum, so I'd really have to creep up on him. I can't tell you how many times I woke up with that thought on my mind and how close I came to trying it. Had I seen him, I knew I would've went through with it, and I know I would've either gotten killed or sent to prison for life. As time went on, I realized it wasn't a smart thing to try and kill a cop. I also knew I couldn't coexist with him in that school

KING BENJAMIN

either. I cut my losses and never went back. Graduation no longer seemed realistic.

TILL DEATH AND BEYOND

I THINK GROWING UP, everybody has somebody that they look up to or maybe even pattern themselves after that person's blueprint. If you have a father in your life that you love and respect, a lot of times he'll be that person. I loved my stepfather a lot, but there was nothing impressive about him to me. He went to work, came home, went to bed. He did take care of home, which looking back on it, he had a lot to be proud of because he was a standup guy in that sense.

I just didn't get much influence from him. The first people that really impressed me were the older guys I ran with. I spent a lot of time with them so I got to see how they handled certain situations and what made them tick. Don was my brother's friend first and also the guy in the cell with him the day we both went to jail. He used to hustle for Wack. I ran with Don and Wack for maybe five years, but the effect they had on my life went so far beyond those years. My whole street mentality came from watching them and how they moved.

After I pretty much gave up on school, I spent a lot of my days on the block watching and learning. I'd get up every day and leave the house like I was going to school, but I would go straight to Don's house. Although Don worked for Wack, he was far from a worker. He was only seventeen at the time and he was just paying the dues that everybody paid to climb the ladder of success. These niggas were like teenage mobsters. They lived their lives doing whatever they wanted to do, and they had no regrets or remorse about it.

KING BENJAMIN

Now, a lot of the guys in my circle lived that way, but what separated these guys was they weren't doing stupid stuff like carjacking people for the sake of joyriding or running up on a nigga taking gym shoes. If it didn't make some real dollars, it didn't make sense to them. The way the story was told to me, Wack got on by robbing a nigga for his Gucci link and he never looked back. He was a true-blue hustler and the strongest link in our chain that held all of us together. Everyone had a mutual love and respect for Wack. He wasn't the oldest, but he was the smartest and the most advanced.

He was stood only about 5' 7 with bowlegs, dark skin with brush waves, and bad acne. Don was tall, light brown with broad shoulders, and built like a quarter back, which would be the position he played very well for little league all of his teenage years. His mom would call him Mr. Cool all the time because of his demeanor. The name fit him more than she realized. I'd never seen Don or Wack in a panic, no matter what was going on. They both had a walk and a presence that said "don't fuck with me." Don was like a big brother and one of my closest friends. Wack would've been what niggas today call the big homey. At age sixteen, I watched these guys like a hawk because it just seemed like they had all the answers and they were doing everything they said they would do.

Don and Wack took a liking to me because they said I had heart. They took me under their wings and gave me guidance. They pointed out all the dumb shit that other niggas were doing and told me to stay away from it. The more I saw how stupid a lot of it was, the more I came around Don every day just to hang out and kick it. He was just glad I listened. There was no money in what the other homies were doing, and it was just a matter of time before they got caught up. The risk wasn't worth the rewards.

After I kept hanging around every day, Don would throw me a few dollars just because he knew I was probably broke. I would stand on the block with him while he hustled and watch

FIGHT OF MY LIFE

his back. Honestly, I would've done it for free because I was learning valuable street lessons every day. I really liked the way these guys thought and what they were teaching me. They taught me how to shoot guns, everything from revolvers to Uzis. They talked to me about grinding, saving money, and watching out for snakes. Most of the other street niggas I knew were just wilding out, they had no discipline. These two guys showed me how to turn nothing into something. One example of Don's discipline always stood out.

Don started hustling for Wack when he was kicked out of all Detroit Public Schools. His mom put him in an all-boy school and they said if he stayed out of trouble for a year, he could come back to regular school. Since there were no girls to impress in an all-boys school, there was no need to get fly every day. Don wore the same Dickies pants and flannel shirt for months every day. It was never dirty or smelly, so I'm assuming he washed it regularly, but he never wore anything else. It got to a point that the neighbor kids would tease him as they came home from elementary school.

This guy would be walking around with a couple grand in his pocket every day, but he wouldn't take off that outfit. Around this same time, Wack would dress down a lot too, just sweatpants and hoodies. I found out later that this was how hard they grind when they had set goals for themselves. Don was turning all the money over to Wack. Wack was investing every dime into a bigger package. On the outside looking in, you wouldn't know any money was being made. Wack rarely drank or smoked but if he did, you better believe he wasn't the one paying for it. He'd have thousands of dollars in his pocket and ask one of his workers to buy him something to eat.

He was stingy on a whole other level, but we learned later there was a method to his madness. I can't paint the picture as if Wack was loved by everyone, because he wasn't. He could be grimy, he could be a shit starter, and he would play you like a pawn if you let him, but he was the one that showed us all how to hustle and how to come up. He was the first one I watched do it play by play. After months of hard work, Wack and Don started to look like the neighborhood drug dealers they were. The went from always bummy to always fresh. Wack bought a Malibu and got it painted then threw some chrome rims on it. He took the backseat out and put fifteen-inch speakers in place of it.

As his operation expanded, his team grew. Although he could round up thirty guys easily if need be, the crew that he hustled with was a lot smaller but twice as dangerous. Wack rolled with real killers, so you never had any doubt that he was one himself. As the money grew, they started to take control of the area, burning down houses and running out competition. I didn't see any of it happen, I just heard about it the next day, and I watched them grow more paranoid as the time passed.

They stopped walking down the main road and Wack started only driving his car at night. It was obvious they had enemies. Don was still only seventeen and living with his mom. It was hard for him to buy anything but clothes and explain where the money was coming from. But the one thing he had was a shitload of guns. You would think these niggas were going to war in Iraq the way they stacked up arsenals. Because they had such an arsenal and because they had a crew of solid dudes on their team, Wack bullied a lot of niggas in the streets but eventually, he ran into some guys that weren't buying it.

As their enemies continued to grow, money kept pouring in, and when the summer came, Wack bought a low-rider truck with a mean paint on it. This was during the time low riders were the shit. He came through the hood bumping Too Short's "Freaky Tales". I remember being a little in awe of how good things were going for them back then. Don still didn't have a car, but he was seeing more money than he'd ever seen in his young life. He was still only seventeen and everyone knew it was just a matter of time before he became his own boss.

FIGHT OF MY LIFE

In the meantime, he was still a student of the game himself, passing down all he learned to me. I was soaking it all up and locking it in. I was still too young or maybe just too inexperienced to do anything with the knowledge, but I was patiently waiting for my time as I listened and learned. I watched how they talked in codes and how they never entered the room and just blurted out shit. Everything was a private conversation, just like the mob. I was there every day, but I couldn't tell the police shit if I was arrested because that's how they moved. Everything was a secret unless it was something I needed to know.

This was before most of the gangster flicks even came out, so this wasn't something they picked up from watching movies; this was them living life. I grew up around real gangsters in every sense of the word. Today, you see guys make a lot of money and even do some gangster things, but you rarely see real gangsters nowadays.

By 1991, about 20 to 30 of the guys I grew up around were locked up. They'd sent most of them to M.T.U in Ionia, Michigan. Don was doing 18 months for a gun charge, but Wack was still on the streets balling. He only had a few dudes on the streets at this time, so most of the time I saw him he was alone. I never tried to work for Wack because he and Don always treated me like I was a boss in training. I never asked and he never offered. Maybe it was because they knew my brother, who was in jail, wouldn't approve. Whatever it was, I went off and began my own journey. As he saw me venture out and start to hustle on my own, he was grinning like a proud father when we were together. Wack didn't teach me things the same way Don did.

Don would teach me verbally while Wack would just say ride with me here and there and show me through exposure. The last time I saw Wack was August of 1991. He had a drop-top Mustang with a blue flip-flop paint on it. It was a real beauty, especially at night. I was in the liquor store and he came in with that signature grin on his face, as if he approved of the

KING BENJAMIN

girl I was with. We slapped fives and kicked it for a minute outside of the store about my brother and Don, who were both still locked up in Ionia.

He asked me a little about the girl I was with, who was standing nearby waiting on me. I told him I was just getting to know her and we said our goodbyes. He hopped in the drop top and blasted the music. He blew the horn as he pulled off, flying up Van Dyke. That would be the last time I saw the big homey. On Labor Day of '91, one of Wack's many beefs finally caught up with him.

He was driving down Vandyke, passing Harper with the top down, when a car pulled up behind his car and started firing shots. He swerved into a bus, which knocked him from the streets and onto the curb of Kettering High School. He died minutes later, right on the front grass of our high school. We all couldn't believe the irony of where he took his last breath. The place we'd raised so much hell. Wack had bullied and underestimated a lot of people along the way. The final lesson he taught me was in death: don't underestimate anyone.

THAT ONE STREET

I LOST WACK WHEN I was sixteen and he was twenty-one. The things I learned from him I still apply to my life to this day. I always tell people the biggest difference between me and all the street niggas I ran with that's no longer here is the simple fact that they didn't live long enough to mature and I did.

I still remember the day that initially pushed me to start hustling. I don't know that I would take that decision back either. One day, I was coming downstairs from my bedroom and found my mom sitting at the dining room table crying with a table covered with bills. When I asked why she was crying, she basically told me that they couldn't pay all this stuff. I think my pops was laid off at the time, or maybe she was. All I remember was things were getting too tight for me to just sit back and let it happen. I already knew where I could make some money. I hung out there all day every day anyway, so it was time I started to capitalize.

My boy Boogie, who was one of my closest friends, had a big brother named Face. Face was hustling out of house that his family owned on the block that I would hang out on every day. I went to Face and asked him to let me work the spot for a day. Just so happened, his workers were about to go on a mini vacation for a day or two. He set me up with a $650 sack and told me that $500 was his and the $150 was mine. That wasn't a bad deal, I thought. I had no idea what I was in for. It wasn't long before he told me just how much money I could

KING BENJAMIN

make off of this $650 sack. He left me at the house all alone to get my sack off. It wasn't even four hours had passed before I was calling him to tell him I was done. Not only was I done, I had way more than $650 in cash, and I only owed $500. A lot of the dime rock sold for twenty to the white customers, which I didn't know until after I started. The white customers made up about thirty-five percent of the clientele. When they came through the door asking for twenties, I didn't really know what to think. But after handing them rocks and seeing they were satisfied, I picked up on it quickly.

Face brought me two more sacks and I ended up hustling until the wee hours of the morning. I'd told my mom I was spending the night at Boogie's house, which was something I really did from time to time. I made so much money, I didn't even know what to do with it. Too much money to tell my mom about. After that night, I would hustle maybe once or twice a week when Face needed me. I made up lies about winning a scratch-off ticket the first time I gave my mom some money. One time, I even told her I found some money on the street.

After a while, Face had so many workers, he didn't need me anymore so I stopped, but by that time, I was already addicted to the money. It was definitely not the end of my hustle run. I just had to find a way to get back in the game. Up until then, I think the most dirt I'd really done was rob somebody with a BB gun for chump change with Boogie. Thinking back, I believe the main reason I did those robberies was the anger I had built up inside of me as I suffered with low self-esteem. I had to release it by making someone else's life hell. Besides helping my mom out, I started to see hustling as an easy way to change the way I was feeling about myself. When I was sixteen, I worked a summer job just long enough to save up a few checks and buy drugs with the money.

I set up shop with Boogie on that one street off Van Dyke. We both had a quarter ounce each. It wasn't much, but it was

36

FIGHT OF MY LIFE

enough to get paid. We flipped the work a few times and I'd give my mom some money here and there, but never enough where I had to explain where I was getting it from. She knew that I had a knack for saving and supposedly still had a summer job. She also knew that I had friends that were legally hustling, doing things like yard work. If I gave her more than $50, I'd say I was working with a friend doing landscaping. It wasn't long before summer was over and my little package dissolved. I couldn't afford to buy more drugs, and I didn't have another way to get the money. Months went by before I was able to re-up again and this time, I went full-fledged hustler.

It was now wintertime and the best time to grind. This block was a drug heaven with addicts swarming through the neighborhood constantly looking for crack and heroin. Boogie's brother still had a crack house on the first block, and my homey, Freaky, had a strip on the middle block to himself. We stood out on the strip and sold our dope because Freaky spent a lot of time in the house on the phone, playing cards, smoking weed, and trying to get some pussy from some girl in the hood. He was one of the first guys around our age on that one street that was getting some money from the dope game.

He was doing so good, he didn't really feel the need to stand out in the cold in the dead of winter, but we did. The money came quickly and before you know it, everybody and they mama had grabbed a sack and joined us on the strip. It went from two or three niggas to ten niggas fighting for sales. Guys would take off running up the block as soon as a car they knew was a customer hit the corner. Then everyone else gave chase. It was madness! A lot of guys got their whole sack snatched by running up on a desperate crackhead with a bag full of rocks dangling from their fists for the world to see. The crackhead would just snatch the bag and stomp the gas.

It even happened to me a couple times, but after that, I learned my lesson. The last time somebody tried to snatch my sack, I had a pistol on me, and I was apparently feeling like the stuntman Evil Knievel. A White girl pulled up in an S10 pickup

KING BENJAMIN

truck. I noticed I didn't see any money in her hand. She asked for two rocks, but she never reached for the forty dollars. I handed her the rocks without thinking but soon as I did, I realized what was about to happen. Before she could put the car in drive, I jumped on the step bar that extended from under that driver's side door.

One hand was on the door and the other had my sack. She tried to pull off with me hanging on, so I punched her in the face. She pulled off anyway and now I'm getting taken for a ride. I punched her again, trying to get her to stop and let me off, but she picked up the speed on me. Now my life was officially in serious danger. She stomped the gas harder, to the point I had to hold on to the door handle with both hands or I was gonna fall. My heart started pounding like a drumroll as I saw parked cars on both sides of the street. I thought she might try to swerve into one of them to get me off the truck.

"Get the fuck off my car!" she screamed.

By now, I'm realizing this was a super stupid thing to do. I pulled my upper body up into the car and tried to choke her, but that only made her swerve, so I stopped. Now we're all the way at the end of the third block.

"Stop the car or I'ma shoot yo' ass!" I yelled.

She stared straight ahead, focused on the road like she hadn't heard a word I said. The drugs had her mind, and she didn't care about death at the moment, only those rocks she'd stolen. She bent the corner as if she was going to take me all the way home with her. I took one hand off the door to reach for my gun. My other hand slipped off the door and I went crashing to the ground. My gun fell out of my waist and went flipping up the street in the opposite direction. When I finally stopped rolling up the block, I looked to see if any cars were coming, about to run me over. Luckily, she had to slow way down to bend the corner so I wasn't hurt, just embarrassed. I swore I'd kill her if I ever saw her again.

FIGHT OF MY LIFE

We continued hustling hard on the strip every day. Boogie and I were just happy to be making money. By now, I'm sure my mom was suspicious about my activity and the money I was giving her, but I think she may have needed it so much that she just prayed I was being honest. I was also gonna have to explain why I wasn't bringing home a report card soon. Meanwhile, Face's spot was doing numbers, but he wasn't happy with his workers. He was looking to replace them.

Face never wanted Boogie selling drugs but at the end of the day, we were gonna do it anyway with or without his approval. It didn't make sense for us to be right down the street standing out in the cold when his brother had a nice warm house that we could sit in and sell drugs, making way more money.

So, one day, he finally asked us to come on down and help him out. We jumped at the chance, knowing he had a huge clientele already. This was big for us. No more chasing cars up the street, no more fighting for customers or standing out in the cold. The money came incredibly easy. We still sold dimes for twenty and kept the extra ten. Once I started working for Face, I was guaranteed to make three to four hundred dollars a day. Around this time, my brother was about to come home on parole.

I kept thinking to myself, wait until my brother gets home and sees how I'm taking care of my business. I can't lie, I loved hustling. I loved how the OGs would see me in the streets and show me love once they knew I was doing my thing. I was always working. My mom was just used to me hanging out on that one street every day way before I started hustling. It was easy for me to just get up and go, saying I was going to hang out with friends without too many questions asked. If I wasn't getting some pussy, I was on the block getting to the money.

Lisa was still my girl, but I never spent much time with her once I started hustling. I spent money but not a lot of time. We made up a lie to her parents about my father owning a

KING BENJAMIN

construction company so she wouldn't have to explain why I always had money. I'd met her parents and she'd met mine, but I doubted they would be meeting each other any time soon. Believe it or not, after a few months of hustling at Face's house, Boogie and I decided to try our hand at a form of pimping as well. We met this prostitute that favored Chili from TLC. She was a drug addict with nowhere to go.

She was making a killing on the hoe stroll and spending a lot of money with us. She seemed to be always there anyway, upstairs getting high. We moved her in and gave her a room, and she agreed to give us every dime she made with the exception of what she needed to keep for the necessities like food and personal hygiene. She also kept the house clean as a whistle and all we had to do was give her a few free rocks here and there to keep her motivated to go out and get money. It was good deal for a while and everybody was happy. Every time she went out and came back, she had a pocket full of money.

After a while, I guess she realized that we were getting over like a fat rat. She was making a lot of money but never had any. By then, we'd gotten comfortable with her. We fell asleep in the house with her and everything. I know you're probably thinking, mmm hmm, y'all was tricking with that crack head too. Honestly, I never did, but I'd be lying if I said I never let an addict perform oral on me. It actually happened several times when I first started, just not that time with that particular addict. One day, she decided to make her move. We always kept rocks on a plate sitting on a coffee table for quick access. Never a lot, just enough to swallow if the police came knocking. We woke up one day and all the rocks were gone and had been replaced with sheetrock. Chili was gone and we never saw her again. That was the beginning and the end of us trying our hand at pimping.

By the time spring rolled around, Boogie and I had stacked up enough money to buy cars, clothes, and anything else we

FIGHT OF MY LIFE

wanted at that stage in our young lives. My brother was home from jail and had decided he was going to try his hand at hustling as well. It wasn't his first time, but this was his first attempt at serious hustling. He'd run into a lump sum of money because his father passed while he was incarcerated, leaving him forty thousand dollars.

He didn't really need to hustle at that point, but he wanted to. Actually, I could've given it up myself if my sole purpose was to help my mom and dad out with the bills. Once he ran into that money, he had to give it to my mom being that he was incarcerated. But she didn't spend any of it unless it was absolutely necessary, so the money was there for him when he got home. But that was his money, not mine. So I kept going.

Black was twenty-one years old with a pocket full of money and a bunch of friends ready to help him spend it all. I never really asked my brother for any money around this time because I didn't need it. I had my own money, but I always thought it would've been nice had he ever offered. So, while I was stacking money, my brother was running through his. He didn't have any experience in buying, cooking, or cutting dope. When he bought cocaine, he cut the rocks so big he wasn't making any profit. He kept buying and selling dope anyway. One time, someone stole an eighth of a kilo from his closet and he went right out and bought another that he probably still wouldn't see any profit from. All of this was happening during my winter grind. I would just hear things and shake my head about it.

People on the outside looking in thought my brother was balling from his hustle. It appeared he was getting money in the streets like never before. He had two or three cars and a crib. In reality, he blew through the money in less than a year when he could've went and got a job and lived good for a lot longer. Forty thousand went a lot further in the early nineties than it does today. When I looked back on it years later, I think Black hustled because everybody else was doing it. When I started hustling it was really out of desperation.

KING BENJAMIN

It was really because my mom was at home with more bills than she could handle. It was because I got tired of seeing her crying because of shutoff notices. Don't get me wrong, I had my own selfish reasons also, but that really was the driving force behind the decision. There were times when my stepfather just didn't have a job. He would always be looking and just couldn't find anything. He really wanted to be a chef, that was his area of expertise, but at this time things just weren't going his way. This was before my brother came into the money, of course. There was no money coming in really, so I stepped up to the plate.

By summer of '93, nobody was worried about bills and no more shut off notices were coming. I felt like I was a grown up even though I was only seventeen. When my eighteenth birthday was approaching, my brother was selling his car and I bought it. It was a 1979 Monte Carlo. It was super clean, had chrome rims and a banging system. I thought I was the shit coming through in it, fresh from head to toe with a pocket full of money. Right after that, Boogie and I hired workers to run the spot for us, even though we still worked for Face.

My self-esteem went through the roof during this time. Because I don't want this book to be a thousand pages, I'll skim through some parts of my life and get to the point without leaving out important details. During this time, my boy Don had come back home and was doing good for himself hustling, but he was on a tether. He was his own boss now and I was doing my thing, so we didn't see each other as much as I would've liked to. Unfortunately, less than six months after he came home, he swallowed a half ounce of cocaine running from cops and died from a drug overdose.

The loss still hurts me to this day. I just knew Don was going to be one of the best that ever did it, but he was not so lucky. He died at nineteen years old. As I began to lose friends, I tried to process what it meant for my own life. I tried to tell myself I would allow them to live through me, and that meant

FIGHT OF MY LIFE

I had to become a huge success. Still, as people around me began to die, I was always very aware of my own mortality.

Once I didn't have to sit in a spot anymore, I started hustling weed on the side while moving around. Everyone on the block smoked weed so again, it was easy money. During this time, Lisa and I started to drift apart. I wasn't spending time with her because I was getting so much attention from other females that my interest started to venture elsewhere. I still cared about Lisa deeply, but I knew it was just a matter of time before we called it quits. All the girls I'd been crushing on were now crushing on me as well. This was a chance to make up for the lackluster high school days. I couldn't just walk away from that opportunity. So that summer, we broke up, but we did remain friends.

I got used to having a little money after a while and it didn't mean that much to me. I was always trying to get more. I didn't have the urge to keep shopping, gambling, or club hopping like a lot of my friends. All the regular hang-ups that slowed most people down in the streets, I didn't have. We were the new hood stars getting money, but I knew that once it was gone, you'd just be the big dummy that fell off. After losing Wack, Don, and a couple others, my focus was to step my game up and get all I could to eventually get out of the game. I knew now that I wasn't guaranteed tomorrow.

I was eighteen years old making more than a thousand a week profits from crack and weed. I had more Air Max and Air Forces than I could count. I even bought my first pieces of jewelry, a diamond pinky ring and another for my ring finger. I was well on my way, but so were the rainy days. A few months after the summer, police had seen enough. They started shutting the block down every day. They started straight harassing everybody, taking us to jail for loitering, drug paraphernalia, and whatever else they could think of. All of a sudden, we were running from police all the time. It came to a point when nobody was making money, and everybody was just catching cases. I stepped away from the block for a while

KING BENJAMIN

before my luck ran out. It wasn't an easy thing to do. I'd gotten used to having money. Now I was spending all the money on daily living. Before I'd turned eighteen, my mom had to finally accept the fact that I was selling drugs, and she basically kicked me out.

I moved in with my brother that summer, but by winter of '93, I was no longer selling drugs and I moved back home. With a lot of free time on my hands, I started working on a rap album. I always wanted to rap, but it seemed I never had time for it. Now I had time and the more I wrote, the better I got. Black and I started working on raps together. It was obvious we were talented by the reaction we'd get from people. My boy Hammer was working on an album also and the more we all talked about doing music, it started to feel like something we could do. But my motivation came and went when I realized I didn't have the money to pay for studio time.

I still continued to write rhymes and freestyle over beats for fun, but what wasn't fun was being as broke as I was. People changed on you the minute they realized you weren't doing so good. I lost contact with a lot of the female friends that had only recently came around when I was getting money. I remember one day when my car was down and I had to take the bus somewhere. I was desperately hoping to not run into anybody, but just my luck, one of the girls that I'd been dating in the summer rode by and burst into laughter. I knew right then I couldn't stay broke much longer. I went crawling back to Lisa and we ended up messing around again, but it didn't last. I was always in a bad mood because I was struggling. This was my first experience with the ups and downs of the game. It was a tough lesson to learn, but then, just like that, one day the lesson was over.

LOOSE CANNON

AFTER SITTING AT HOME WATCHING my stash dwindle down to nothing in a few short months, one day I picked up the phone and called Boogie. Boogie called Face and we all came to an agreement that it was time to get back to work. Technically, our spot never got raided, so we were confident that we had let the block cool off long enough. This time when we opened again, Face was right there grinding with us. I think he did that so the customers would see his face and know that he was still running the show. It worked out as planned and business picked up quickly. We had the whole block to ourselves for a while, and that meant more money for the three of us. Freaky was out of town hustling in Springfield, Illinois. A couple of guys quit hustling as soon as they caught their first case but as time went on, the rest of them slowly began to make their way back to the block.

Black was broke now and hustling in the hood with my man Chaz, but they did more arguing than hustling. I knew it wouldn't last long, so I told my brother I would talk to Face to see if he could come help us out on the block. By that time, the block was back to normal and there was more than enough money coming in for everybody to eat. Face agreed and Black joined us shortly after. Around this same time, Face hit my man Jack with some work.

Jack used to work under Freaky but since Freaky was out of town, he'd been out of a job. Jack the Maniac, as we called him, was a good hustler and he moved work wherever he went. At this time, Face was making the majority of the money on

KING BENJAMIN

the block and whoever wasn't with us was just getting our table scraps. But nobody was complaining because we were all just happy to be making money again. Everybody on the block knew about the time I got dragged up the street in the truck by the crackhead that tried to rob me. I definitely never forgot about it.

It was a rainy night, months and months later, and a black truck pulled up to the house with two white passengers, one male and one female. Nobody knew the male driver, but Boogie, Jack, and I knew who the passenger was. It was her. I couldn't believe after what she did, she thought I'd just forget her face. She had money in her hand this time, but I didn't give a shit about the money. She could've killed me, and she had stolen from me.

"Don't nobody serve her," I whispered as I dipped off into the house to get my Glock.

Face didn't hear me, so when I came back out to the porch, I saw him leaned off in the car about to give her some dope. I rushed off the porch with my pistol in hand. I had every intention of shooting her right in the head.

"Move, Face," I growled, seeing red now near the bottom step.

My crew saw the barrel of the gun and rushed out of the line of fire. No form of reasonable thoughts crossed my mind as I aimed at the passenger side window and started firing shots. I fired three or four times. It was raining heavy so as the driver tried to peel off, the tires spun out and he splashed mud and water all over my clothes and in my face. The last few shots I fired blindly in their direction. By the time I could see again, the truck was halfway up the block. Everybody was saying they believed I'd shot the woman, but I knew I missed them both. It was only after I'd reacted, probably the next day, that I realized I could've easily shot and killed that lady that night.

FIGHT OF MY LIFE

This was just the first time God decided to spare my life. Luckily for me, he was just getting started, because so was I.

When I was young, I always reacted without thinking things through. This is one of the reasons we have so many young black males incarcerated for violent crimes today. We don't think things through. We react instead of responding, and we react with raw, unfiltered emotions. That incident was just the beginning of a long string of wild and unruly nights on our part. It seemed like after that night, my crew just became reckless as hell.

They started beating up the customers on a daily basis, especially Jack. He'd beat a fiend for ten minutes over five dollars. Jack and Black quickly became drinking and gambling buddies. A few weeks after the incident with the white girl, I shot a fiend in the foot because he wouldn't buy my drugs. I wasn't really intending to shoot him. I aimed at the concrete and shot but I ended up actually hitting him. To this day, I believe I really broke the concrete with the bullet and that's what hit him in the foot, but he still claims I shot him. Like I said, I wasn't thinking anything through. Lucky for him, he was only grazed. He hopped away and came back a few days later to buy from me.

By 1994, everybody in the hood knew I was a loose cannon. I was only 140 pounds soaking wet with a major chip on my shoulder. I knew I had to earn my respect in the hood or niggas would try me based on my size alone. A nigga with some size on 'em would look at me and just assume he'd make light work on my little ass. No matter how many fights I won, I was always slept on because of my size. So, I stayed scrapping, but I also stayed strapped and ready to prove a point. Don't play with me. If you weren't in my circle you didn't get to shoot a fair one with me. My reputation as a shooter grew quickly. One day, Face pulled up on me and told me his connect was looking to pay somebody to do a hit. I don't know why he picked me, because any one of us would've gladly taken the job.

KING BENJAMIN

I think it might've been because I knew how to keep quiet about things. I wasn't big on talking or bragging about dirt. Whatever it was, he said the pay was twelve thousand, and I didn't hesitate to take on the job. Apparently, another dude had already fumbled the job, so we had to use caution. We met up with the plug that night in McDonald's parking lot. This was the first time I'd ever laid eyes on the plug. He pulled up in a black Lexus and he glanced at me but didn't say anything. He got out and walked over to the driver's side of Face's car.

"Is this the guy that's gonna do it?" he asked.

Face nodded.

"Okay, follow me," he said.

I'd heard a lot about Face's connect. He was a young, rich, self-made millionaire from drug selling. If that didn't give us motivation, nothing would. As we rode to the location, Face explained more details about the situation. He told me we were headed to the target's house and would wait for him to come home from work. Out of curiosity, I asked where did the dude work. Face told me this nigga delivered pizzas for a living. My mind started spinning like crazy.

Why would a million-dollar nigga have beef with the pizza delivery guy? Did he fuck up the order that bad? Give a nigga food poisoning? Before I finished thinking, it got even deeper. Face revealed that the pizza guy was fucking the plug's girl. The plug started off just planning to burn the guy's house down but at some point, his anger escalated and now he wanted him dead. Again, my mind was spinning. *Why the hell is his girl creeping with pizza boy? Is it revenge? Lack of attention?* It really didn't matter to me though. Back then, for twelve G's I would've killed the pizza boy and the UPS man as a bonus.

We arrived on the block and parked down the street from the target's house. The connect was maybe two blocks down, parked far enough to not be linked to us if something went wrong. I sat my Glock on my lap, waiting for them to give me

FIGHT OF MY LIFE

the go ahead. I was thinking about the fact that this would be my first murder. I was a little nervous, but I was positive I was about to make a bloody mess of the pizza boy. As time passed, my mind drifted to all the things I was going to do with the money.

At no time did I ever think about backing out or even feeling like it wasn't a good idea. More time passed and Face and I began to get sleepy and downright bored. After about four hours, the connect called and said he didn't believe the target was coming home. He said we could try another day. We met up in another parking lot and he gave me a hundred dollars for my time and told us we could try again soon. They never asked me to do the hit again.

LESSON LEARNED

WHEN I FIRST STARTED TO distance myself from Lisa, there was a beautiful, model tall girl that was giving me a lot of attention at the time. She was a big reason for our breakup. When I was officially single, we went on a couple dates and I immediately fell hard for her. She was the best eye candy I'd ever come across at that point in my life. In total, we only dated for five or six months but in that time, I probably spent more money on her than I'd spent on Lisa the entire time we'd been dating. This chick was a seductress and honestly, had too much game for me.

I thought if I showered her with gifts, she would only have eyes for me but every time I turned around, I was hearing things. She never fell for me the way I fell for her. She was basically with me for the financial benefits, but I was too wide open to notice. After we broke up, she started dating Freaky, which I had no problem with. I had come to realize we just weren't meant to be; plus, she and Freaky were just a better fit. They went on to have a kid together. Eventually, Freaky started to go out of town to hustle and left the girl with too much time on her hands.

We began to talk on the phone here and there, but it never led to anything more than that. Since she was always in the neighborhood and on the block, people on the outside looking in noticed the change in our relationship. I was always cordial with her, but now things had gotten flirtatious between us again. I still had a thing for the girl, and in my eyes, she had chosen me before she ever chose Freaky, so there was nothing

FIGHT OF MY LIFE

foul about it. Although I knew this girl was nothing more than my karma for treating Lisa so badly, I couldn't break the habit of entertaining her.

Soon word got out that Freaky had a girl he was living with out of town. I only heard about it when his girl in Detroit told me. Around the same time, Freaky got wind of how close me and his girl had become as of late. To make a long story short, Freaky blamed me, believing that I was the one that ratted him out about having a girl out of town. I couldn't believe it. Of all the shit I'd been accused of, I was never accused of breaking that kind of code.

Although Freaky and I were friends, he'd gotten a name like Freaky because he was known to creep around with other niggas' girls. I also wasn't breaking any codes by entertaining his baby mother knowing what he would've done had the shoe been on the other foot. There weren't too many niggas' girls he hadn't slept with. But giving up information on a nigga to get his girl was just pathetic and something I'd never stoop to. I was shocked and caught completely off guard when he came back in town and tried to confront me about snitching on him. I was walking up the street and he rushed out of his mom's house and ran up on me with his fist balled up.

"What's up, nigga? You wanna see me or something?" he challenged.

"The fuck you talking about?" I asked, genuinely confused.

Freaky went on to accuse me of telling his girl information I had no access to. I didn't know anything about his personal life that went on out of town until she told me. But here he was, getting further in my grill. We were nose to nose now, and there was no question about whether Freaky wanted to fight. When I'd finally heard enough, I cocked back and socked Freaky in the face. He returned with a blow of his own but after that, I don't remember getting hit again.

KING BENJAMIN

As I connected with blow after blow, I realized I was much faster than he was. On top of that, I'd been accused of the worst kind of betrayal, and I was angry. After about sixty seconds of scrapping, Freaky had enough. I saw his eye swelling fast as our friends stepped in to break it up. Freaky took the L better than I would have. He eventually apologized when he found out the truth.

We patched our relationship up later on that year and things went back to normal with us. I found out later it was one of the dudes that was actually out of town with him that was telling the girl everything. He was creeping around trying to get with her when he came in town. I was such a live wire at the time, I realized things could've really turned out bad for myself or Freaky, all over a misunderstanding. More importantly, I realized how one woman had almost turned three men against each other. I distanced myself from his girl for good after that.

G-BLOCK

EVEN WITH ALL OF OUR wilding out on the block, business was still booming. I was making about fifteen hundred a week profit at this point. Summer rolled around again and Boogie and I bought new whips. I bought a Regal and got a white candy paint on it then threw on some chrome Dayton's. I bought a whole new wardrobe and a bunch of sneakers. I started running with some of my old friends that I'd stopped hanging with because Don suggested I should. I should point out there was never any bad blood between any of us. Some of these dudes were Don's blood relatives and they lived right down the street from one another. He just knew they were on a road to destruction and didn't want me to sink with the ship.

By now, everyone was growing up, had been to prison and back, and was getting money in the game. Most of us had left all the petty shit behind us. A few of my friends had developed serious gambling habits and it was always a dice game on the block. I worked too hard for my money to gamble it away, plus I always heard about how my biological father was a compulsive gambler. I stayed away for those reasons, but I'd do a little side betting here and there.

The dice games in the hood were always the cause of a lot of conflict. We were still all very young, but respect meant more to us than money even back then. Guys were willing to catch a life sentence if they felt disrespected in a dice game. Their pride just wouldn't let them walk away. I could write a

KING BENJAMIN

book on the incidents that went down at dice games alone, and I was always right there whether I was gambling or not.

Jack was a huge gambler, and he would get into an altercation almost every time he lost. He'd snatch his money back if he thought you were soft, and if he couldn't do that, he'd take his anger out on the customer that came to the spot by pulverizing one of them for one petty reason or another. There came a time when Face was fed up with all the unruliness. Eventually, we started losing business because my crew was always assaulting the customers. One day, Face came on the block and fired everybody except for me and Boogie. I totally understood it was just business, but I was kinda upset that he'd fired my brother.

My whole crew was unemployed now and looking for work. After a few days passed, I started to see this as an opportunity to step out on my own. I'd been working for Face for two years now. It was time to take things to the next level. I started talking to Jack about doing something. He was pissed and thinking along the lines of taking all of Face's customers. I was thinking along the lines of taking everybody's customers. I had enough money saved to go off on my own. I decided to go with my gut, quit working for Face, and copped my own work. I bought an eighth of a kilo and hit Jack and his uncle off with an ounce each. They started slanging right out the back window of the house they lived in.

All the fiends knew them and were used to them. It was a smooth and easy transition and after about two weeks, we realized we were sitting on a gold mine. See, as much as people didn't appreciate being assaulted and bullied, we were the guys in the trenches. We were the faces to the brand. Face was never around anymore, so when he tried to replace the old crew with a new one, the customers decided they'd rather deal with the people they knew. There were so many more of them that had never been beat up and had nothing but good experiences with us. It turned out to be one of the best decisions I'd ever made.

FIGHT OF MY LIFE

Jack's mother was still living in the house they were hustling out of at the time. Once we saw that our plan would work, we quickly moved her out and turned the house into a twenty-four-seven trap house. Right then, I told Jack and his uncle to start saving their money. I didn't want them working for me if they didn't have to. It was obviously going to be enough money coming for everyone to be their own boss. The spot was literally an overnight success. Once people were allowed to come to the house anytime, day or night, they came in flocks.

Three weeks in, we were doing three and four thousand a night. I was already used to selling three and four thousand a night in drugs, but the big difference now was that the money was all mine. I told my brother to come and join us because once again, there was plenty money for everybody. I was making four hundred dollars off of each ounce, and I was selling at least three ounces a day. That wasn't bad for a nineteen-year-old kid.

So Black joined us and Jack came up with the name G-Block to separate us from the other two blocks. That name fit at the time because we were definitely the most gangsta of the three. We were the only real threat to anybody else in the neighborhood at that time because we didn't hesitate to come through and throw lead if we had problems. Even though we were doing so good, every block was getting money. At that time, the whole block was doing a good ten thousand a day. Nobody cared who was getting the most because it was so much coming every day.

But the thing I later realized was when you getting money that fast, you don't think about the fact that it's gonna be over one day. Before long, everyone on G-Block had their own bag. Everyone was copping at least an eighth of a kilo and some days, you could run through an eighth the same day you got it.

Sometimes, we would be the only ones on the whole block with dope. So that meant instead of the three or four thousand

KING BENJAMIN

we usually made, we'd make the whole ten. There was absolutely no reason for me to still be sitting in a spot selling my own dope at this point, but I did it because I didn't care about a dope case. That was my routine. I went to work every day like I had a job.

I had money to either beat the case or at the max, get probation. I'd never been charged with a felony so any case I caught would be a first offense. While I was stacking money, my partners were running through it. They'd go to gambling parties and lose five thousand in one night. And they did it because they knew they could make it right back.

All they had to do was call the connect, get some work on consignment, and be right back on in a week or two. But after watching this continuing trend, I started to distance myself from my crew. I didn't want any of these bad habits rubbing off. To me, they were drinking too much, partying too hard, and gambling way too much. I would get me hotel room with a Jacuzzi and chill with my lady friends. That was my idea of a good time. I was completely satisfied with having a pocket full of money and a couple women in my life that I enjoyed spending time with. Eventually, everybody started looking at me like I was acting funny because I kept to myself.

It wasn't that, I was just thinking bigger and I realized they weren't doing that anymore. They'd gotten comfortable with the little money we were making, but I wanted much more. I was saving and penny pinching, trying to become a rich hood legend like the ones before me. I didn't really have a plan to exit the game, I just knew it took a lot of money to get out and still maintain the same lifestyle. Although I had getting out of the game in the back of my mind, it was a long-term goal that was far, far away.

Since its creation, Jack always talked about how thorough G-Block was and at the time, I believed it to be true. We were definitely the hardest working and the most violent team on the block. I knew my brother and I would go the distance in a

FIGHT OF MY LIFE

real war. I knew Jack's drunk uncle would fold, but I figured every crew had one weak link whether they knew it or not. But I always thought Jack the Maniac was just that. I always thought he would represent that name no matter the situation. Most people thought he was the toughest goon in our clique. That was because he was the most aggressive but at the same time, he brought us the most problems. I soon found out he wasn't what he seemed.

The first time was when we were beefing with this dude Feezy that had a lot of brothers. His brothers didn't want any problems, but Feezy wouldn't back down so he tried to become a one-man army. The beef started because Feezy, in a clear and bold violation, set up shop right across the street from Face's spot. This was when we all worked for Face. He flagged down cars with blatant disrespect for us, trying to serve our customers. This only went on for about a day and a half until we put a stop to it. We got the word that he was carrying a Tech-9 with a thirty-round clip in his coat, so we needed to move with caution.

We ignored him all that day, waiting for nightfall. He wasn't making any money because the customers wouldn't stop for him, but this was about principle. There were four of us in the house and we all had pistols, except Face, who had a Street Sweeper. We didn't really have a plan, but we knew something had to be done. When nightfall rolled around, most of the streetlights were out and we heard someone whistling. We looked outside and spotted Feezy and his little brother in the same spot as yesterday. Jack opened up the door and walked across the street to confront him, and the rest of us came out behind him and positioned ourselves on the porch or the sidewalk.

"You wanna buy something?" I heard Jack bark aggressively.

"What nigga?" Feezy growled back.

KING BENJAMIN

"You heard me. Fuck you out here whistling for, you wanna buy something?" Jack repeated.

"I'm just tryna get money like everybody else," Feezy replied.

"Not here you not. Get the fuck on!"

"Man, y'all niggas ain't on shit. Y'all don't own this block."

Jack pulled out on him before he could finish the sentence. He opened fire and Feezy took cover, leaving his brother to fend for himself. I'd already had my hand on my weapon tucked in my waistline. Once the shooting started, I pulled out and started to unload in Feezy's direction as well. After that, everybody started shooting, but we were literally shooting in the dark. Feezy ran behind the house he was in front of and pulled out the Tec-9. I couldn't see him, but boy could I hear his ass.

He let off round after round, returning fire. I ran out of bullets and took cover to reload. As I ran in the house to reload my weapon, I could hear bullets pinging on the house and ricocheting off the front porch. I thought his clip would never run out of bullets. I knew at least two of my homeboys were still outside, which was what motivated me to run towards the bullets instead of ducking and hiding.

I fumbled around with the bullets with nervous adrenaline flowing through my body. I was moving so fast, I somehow got half the clip in and popped the spring, spilling all the bullets in the clip back out on the floor.

"Fuck!" I shouted.

By the time I loaded the clip again, I crawled out on the porch, staying low as possible. Feezy had just finally stopped shooting. I raised up and fired in the direction I thought he was hiding, but I still couldn't see much because of the streetlights. After I let off a few more rounds and Feezy didn't return fire, we took off looking for him.

FIGHT OF MY LIFE

Jack and I took off on foot while Face and Boogie jumped in the ride. We searched for a while with no luck. Although we didn't find Feezy that night, he found Jack the next morning. He rode up the block with a female driving a big body Lincoln while he hid ducked down in the passenger side with the seat leaned all the way back. As he passed the house, Jack just so happened to be sitting on the front porch. Feezy raised up and fired. He shot Jack's hat clean off his head but didn't hit him. Jack stumbled off the porch and returned fire.

A few days later, they would run into each other again and another shootout ensued. Everyone was in agreement that Feezy had to die. We got a stolen whip and a couple of AK-47s from Face and went hunting for him that same night. I remember us sitting around the next night smoking and drinking, getting our grind on like it was any other day. Around ten pm, we were ready to ride but before we could, our young homey Slim came banging on the front door in a rage. We quickly let him inside to find out what had happened.

"Man, these hoe ass niggas across the tracks just pulled guns on me and shot at Rick's car," he said, excited and angry.

He was about as upset as you'd expect a person to be who'd just had their life put in danger. This was our lil' homie. On top of that, we were all buzzed up and had enough guns in the house to start a war with the whole neighborhood. You can guess what happened next. We piled in the stolen car and drove to the location where the incident had taken place.

Jack was driving as we bent the corner. It was nice outside, and everyone was out mingling in a crowd outside in the streets. As the crowd split in half to let us pass by, Slim spotted his targets and we started shooting. It sounded something like a war movie with all those guns going off at the same time. When we stopped shooting, the car had only moved a few feet. We sped off as Slim continued recklessly unloaded the chopper. When we got to the corner of the block, we spotted police cruising right past. Jack didn't panic, he just waited to

KING BENJAMIN

see what they would do. I personally thought my life was over. Once they drove by, he bent a few corners as fast as humanly possible. Nobody wanted to look back and see if we were being followed until we made it to the freeway. Once we made it to the freeway, I let out a long sigh.

To this day, I'll never understand how the police didn't get on us that night. My only theory is they knew it was us shooting and knew they were outnumbered and outgunned, so they played it safe. We drove to Highland Park and chilled there for a while, letting things cool down. After a while, we ditched the stolen car and went back to the block. I found out later that no one was seriously injured that night. But it was crazy how we started out the day with one goal and ended going in a completely different direction.

After that incident, we didn't see Feezy for a long time. He didn't pop back up until we'd left Face and started doing our own thing. I think by then we were getting so much money, nobody wanted to risk losing it all going to war all over again. Feezy was broke and didn't seem like a threat at first. But one day, I ran into Feezy and it was just me and him. He was riding behind me in his truck. I put my gun on my lap and pulled over. He pulled over behind me. I put my gun in my waist and got out. He stayed in the car. I stood firmly on the front porch of a crackhead's house with my arms folded, waiting for him to make a move. It was broad daylight and everybody on the block was watching nervously to see what would happen next.

Instead of throwing our young lives away, we started to talk. It wasn't exactly a peace talk, but it was better than shooting and killing each other. We both had our hands on our weapons the entire time. But when nothing happened, that was the closest we'd ever come to squashing this beef. One thing I can say about Feezy was he never backed down and he never bitched up. It could've easily gone another way that day, but we both just managed to realize it wasn't worth it.

FIGHT OF MY LIFE

So for a while, we were able to coexist in the hood without incident. That was until the day Jack and Feezy bumped heads in the liquor store. Someone bumped someone else and just like that, it was on again. The story I heard, it sounded like Jack escalated the situation. I wasn't there, but it wasn't hard to believe because that was usually the case. It was the middle of the summer and we were playing cowboys and Indians again.

I wasn't happy about it, but I always had my people back through whatever. We shot up Feezy's crack house and chased his workers away. We chased his younger brother out of the neighborhood as well. Soon, another shootout occurred that I wasn't involved in, and Jack got shot in the foot. Feezy disappeared for a while again and Jack was on crutches for a few weeks. Now I was just angry because this was making us look bad. He was only one guy and it was three of us involved in this beef, not including Jack's uncle. I told Jack it was time to put a stop to this once and for all. The streets were watching and this dude wasn't going away. That's when I realized my dog wasn't who I thought he was. Jack turned and looked me in my eyes.

"I understand all of that, but I'm not ready to do life in prison," Jack said, taking me by surprise.

I couldn't believe my ears.

"Well, I'm not saying go shoot 'em in the face in front of the whole world, but we gotta get him out the way," I explained.

He acted as if he understood the urgency of the situation but after that, he never made move on Feezy, and never brought it up again. Day after day went by with no mention of the situation that needed to be handled. If I brought it up, he brushed it off. I wasn't the one who got shot, so if it wasn't a sense of urgency to them, it became less of a sense of urgency for me. I wasn't going to go avenge someone else that was able bodied to put in their own work. I realized I wasn't running

KING BENJAMIN

with killers like I thought. When it really came down to it, Jack was just a guy pumped up on a lot of liquid courage that got away with throwing his weight around for a number of years. I never really forgave Jack for sparking that beef back up and not finishing it. That put a huge dent in our friendship. I stopped representing G-Block after that and started representing myself.

IT'S A WAR GOING ON OUTSIDE

I STARTED HANGING AROUND BOOGIE a lot more after realizing Jack wasn't the man I'd believed him to be. Boogie and I were still really good friends, we just didn't see each other as much when we stopped being in business together. It felt good being around someone I considered my equal. We were both doing good for ourselves at a young age and we both wanted much more than we had. Not only was Boogie the only one that matched my ambition, but he was also the only person I was friends with before the hustling. Once again, the G-Block crew had started beating up all the customers, which in time started to really slow down business. Meanwhile, my plug was trying to hit me off with a half a brick on consignment.

There were too many people eating off this one house for business to ever be slow. I was only a few coins away from coping a whole brick without any consignment, but business was down dramatically. I didn't even want to put the cash I had upfront and get the rest on consignment because I feared being stuck with a slow-moving kilo of cocaine and an impatient plug calling my phone every other day. See, back then, I didn't know much about venturing outside of the hood. I moved all my package on one block so when things slowed down, I became stagnated. Boogie and I came up with a plan to cop a kilo together. We'd both put up half the money and we would sell it on the first block out of the house I started hustling in at sixteen.

KING BENJAMIN

I would leave G-Block to Jack, my brother, and Jack's uncle to do whatever they pleased. Jack and my brother were still really close, so I knew that's where he wanted to be. I wasn't feeling it anymore, so it only made sense to go where I was comfortable. I didn't even care about the fact that I was leaving a place I had total control to go back to space that I didn't. The fact was I didn't have total control because I couldn't stop them from beating up loyal customers, and I didn't want to fallout with people I genuine loved, especially my own brother. It might sound like a step backwards, but all the money had shifted from the end of the block back to the front because of the likelihood of getting seriously injured dealing with G-Block.

Face and Boogie were making a killing and Boogie was inviting me to join them again. He was my best friend, and it just felt right that we should be getting money together. My other boy Sal was doing seven years for an attempted murder, so as far as friendship went, this guy was the only nigga on the streets I would've went to war for at this time. So, after having a long talk with Boogie, I went and had a long talk with Black.

I told him I wouldn't be using the house anymore and that he should take advantage of my absence. I had a few ounces left to sell before Boogie and I went to cop the kilo. Boogie and Face were now hustling from another spot that was almost directly across the street from the old house. After talking to my brother, I walked down to the first block.

I hadn't seen my homie Freaky since he fell off. He was hustling in Springfield and it had really worked out for him for a while. He'd bought an Impala with a mean paint on it then put hydraulic switches and Dayton's on it. That was around summer of '95 when switches were still the shit. Now it was summer of '96 and somebody had broken into Freaky's house and stolen everything. A whole kilo and all the cash. It was hard for him to bounce back. When I walked in, I saw Freaky sitting on the couch with a bunch of brown hash and weed on the

FIGHT OF MY LIFE

table. I hadn't ever seen hash before that day, so I was never curious about it.

During this time, I smoked a lot of weed and I was a drinker, but that was all I ever wanted or needed. I don't know why I had the urge to try this hash, but I did. Freaky rolled up a box of blunts laced with hash and we went to the store for some liquor. As the blunts began to float around, I was instantly higher than I'd ever been. I didn't even make it past the second blunt. Freaky, being the comedian of our circle, started cracking jokes that had my stomach in knots. Then Face came in and the two of them started going at each other.

I laughed so hard I was crying. I was having such a good time that night I never even did any hustling but looking back, it was such a pivotal moment. It was literally the calm before the disastrous storm. After that night, nothing was ever the same. I remember thinking to myself the next morning when I awakened that this was what it was supposed to be like when you and your friends were getting money. Lots of laughs, lots of a smiles, and lots of love for one another. That's what I felt that night. I just knew I was back where I belonged, but boy was I wrong.

The next day was Sunday. Face and Boogie didn't hustle on Sundays so that meant I had the house all to myself, and it was banging like a Chick-fil-A drive thru. Boogie came through later just to kick it with me. I asked him how Face feel about me did being back at the house hustling my own drugs.

"Why would he care?" Boogie said.

Then I remembered that they never wanted me to leave anyway. It was a decision I'd made on my own. I figured Boogie was probably right, but when Face came to the block the next day, he seemed a little upset. He went to the old house across the street while Boogie and I were hustling. As time went on, I noticed he hadn't come over and said anything to either of us. A little more time passed, and Face called Boogie across the street to the old house and they began to argue. I

KING BENJAMIN

knew it was about me, and I realized for the first time that Boogie hadn't ever mentioned the part about us going into business again with his brother.

As the arguing continued, I decided I wasn't going to just sit around while they argued about me right in front of my face. I walked across the street, and as I was walking up, Face looked at me and scowled.

"What the fuck you want?" he barked, looking at me, disgusted.

"Look, if it's a problem, we can talk about it," I suggested.

"Naw, ain't shit to talk about. You can take yo' ass back down to G-Block," Face replied with an authority I'd never heard in his tone.

"But who the fuck you think you talking to?" I questioned calmly.

At this point, I wasn't really that upset, even though Face was. I just thought he had the wrong impression of my intentions.

"I'm talking to you, little nigga. Take yo' hoe ass back down there to G-Block," he ordered louder.

My eyes grew big with disbelief. Shock was not a strong enough word. I was astounded. Stunned into momentary silence. This dude couldn't have been talking to me. No way did he just try to chastise me like I was punk, a nobody.

"Really dog?" I finally replied with confusion all over my face.

"Say something else, I'ma blow your shit out," he growled.

I'll never forget those exact words as he sat there with a BB gun rifle in his hand, playing with the lever. This was my best friend's brother. This was the guy that introduced me to the game. This was someone I always loved and respected, considered family, and had always shown me nothing but respect. It broke my heart to look in his eyes and see there was

FIGHT OF MY LIFE

no love for me there. Worse than that, I realized at some point Face had stopped respecting me. As I stated before, respect was everything in my hood.

I'm still 140 pounds at the time. I didn't know if Face really wanted to fight, but I knew that he was twice my size and even if we fought, no matter the outcome, I was still probably gonna shoot him for the disrespect. I wasn't afraid to fight him. I was too angry to fight him. Too angry to allow him to call me out of my name and take a swing at me. I knew I was everything Face wasn't. I walked off without another word spoken between us. Face didn't respect me. But as I jumped in my SS Monte Carlo, I didn't want Face's respect after that exchange. I wanted his life. Words should never hurt as much as they did in that moment. I opened up the door to my soul and let the devil in.

"I'm killing that bitch," I told myself as I stabbed off up the block, going straight to grab my pistol.

I'd taken all my guns from G-Block to a female's house I was seeing. When I arrived at her house, I went in and grabbed the first gun I saw in the pistol box, a revolver. As I grabbed the gun and walked out without a word, I thought for a split second about going back to call Face out to shoot a fair one. I quickly tossed the thought aside. I had to make Face eat lead for this. See, the thing about my block was, sometimes you couldn't just square up and box about every situation and that be the end of it.

If it was a situation like Freaky, about a chick or even a dice game, then it could've possibly gone another way. But this was about my livelihood, blocks, territory, and the name I'd made for myself the past few years. Taking an L wasn't even an option when you know your next meal depends on a victory. If I'd called him out for a fair one and got my ass whooped, my point would've been proven and I would've had a hard time eating on the block after that. I would've had to shoot him anyway just to keep my name in good standing.

KING BENJAMIN

Subconsciously, there was a fear factor that had crept inside of me. The fear that my entire reputation was at stake. This is why there's so many young black men dying in the inner city. There's enormous pressure to keep the name you earned in the streets from going sour.

In the streets, sometimes it's not about being afraid to take a L. It's about the respect you could lose from taking that L. But none of that registered as I drove back to the block with full intentions of taking Face's life so everyone knew I was still not to be played with. It was just about to get dark when I made it back to the neighborhood. I drove up from the opposite end of a one way to implement the element of surprise. I still had the same amount of anger inside of me as when I drove off. There were a few more people out on the porch now, but I spotted Face in almost the same exact spot.

By the time he looked up and spotted my car in front of the house, I was shooting at his head. He didn't even have the presence of mind to duck, he just froze in shock then balled up like a turtle trying to hide in his shell. I let the car come to a complete stop as I fired off every round, and the sound of gunfire echoed up and down the block. I drove off on an adrenaline rush like no other I'd felt before. I just knew my name would never be tampered with again when word got out that I'd come through and dropped Face so brazenly. By the grace of God and my terrible aim, Face survived without a scratch, but now the beef was on and it was on sight. I'd put every person that was on that porch's life in danger, and I was ready to do it all over if need be.

Word quickly traveled through the hood about the incident. That's how I knew I hadn't killed him. If I had, I probably would've been in jail before midnight. People started blowing up my phone telling me they heard I shot at Face, but I didn't care to hear it. I wanted to hear that Face was dead. Of course, had I actually killed him, this would've been the end of my story. Someone on the block would've given me up to the

FIGHT OF MY LIFE

police and I would've went away to jail, end of story. But that's not what happened. That was only the beginning and from that point on, it was all about gunplay.

See, the thing that pissed me off the most was that I knew Face wasn't a tough guy. He was a hustler, not I gangsta. I was a real live bang yo' ass on sight gangsta that had put in work and earned my stripes. Face was borderline soft, and I'd put my life on the line to defend his spot for years. I felt insulted, disrespected, and betrayed. After I went home and reloaded and grabbed a second gun, I came back to the block that same night. It was completely deserted now. By then, the whole block knew it was about to be on and had taken cover.

I drove around for a while looking for Face. It took me a long time to leave the neighborhood. I wanted everyone to see me on the prowl, still trying to get it popping after what I'd done. I wanted people to tell him I was still looking for him. I wanted Face terrified to step foot in the hood. That was my biggest mistake. When you back someone in a corner, they had no choice but to fight or lay down and die.

The next day, I finally sat down with my brother and told him what happened. He felt the same way I did and basically agreed that Face was too soft to try and grandstand in that manner. We both felt that there had to be some repercussions for his actions, and we started to plan for what would happen next. For a few days, the block stayed empty. I'd wake up with plans to murder each day. As time went by, my conscience started to tug at me. I started drinking earlier than normal for liquid courage, just because I knew what I was about to do that night and I knew the risks of it going wrong. After about four days, niggas started surfacing in the hood again. This time, I had Black with me. When I reached the hood, I decided I didn't want to try and pull up the same way again because they'd probably be looking for that.

I'd only bought my car a month before. The paint was so bright even with no lights on you could still see it coming

KING BENJAMIN

blocks away. I knew I shouldn't have been in my car doing this in the first place, but I hadn't been thinking clearly all week. I was a twenty-year-old ball of fury. All I had was my rage, and the drinking only crippled my decision-making skills more. I drove through a vacant lot that put me right in front of Face's spot. I knew he couldn't stay away for too long because he needed to make money. I didn't care about money at that time, I just wanted Face dead. Once I shot at him, I had to go full force because I knew he had enough money to get me gone.

I spotted his truck, but no one was outside. I wasn't about to waste bullets shooting up a house, so I drove past. After that, we drove around trying to decide our next move. I was feeling like I had the upper hand because I was on the offense. I was dead wrong. As we bent a corner that eventually led to a dead end but turned into an alley, I saw headlights flashing coming up behind me extremely fast. It didn't take long for me to realize it was that truck. A second later, my instincts kicked in.

I tried to stomp that gas as the distinct sounds of an AK-47 assault rifle started ringing off. A second smaller gun started firing simultaneously as my life flashed before my eyes. Because they were behind us, there was nothing we could do to defend ourselves except duck. I drove past the turn and towards the dead end while my head was down, which meant I could see where the alley was ahead. I continued driving with my head down on the steering wheel, pressing the gas to the floor. I could hear bullets hitting the car and shattering my windshield. I tried swerving left or right to keep from giving them an easy target. I finally reached the dead end, but I didn't look up to see where I was going because they were still shooting. My car just kept rolling down an alley until I ran into a tree.

Realizing I wasn't injured, I immediately got out and started returning fire. The shooters were at the opposite end of the alley quite a distance away, which made it hard to aim and

FIGHT OF MY LIFE

hit someone, but shooting back kept them from coming any closer. The truck hit reverse and started backing out up the street until it was no longer in sight. I realized my brother never got out and started bussing his gun, which wasn't like him. I rushed to my driver's side in a panic. I looked in and saw he was slightly slumped forward.

"You alright, bro?" I called out frantically.

"Naw, I'm hit," he managed weakly.

My heart sank.

"Where?"

"In my back," he said.

My heart sank even lower, pounding like never before. I ran around to his side and opened the door. I lifted his shirt and couldn't see a thing. I thought maybe he was just banged up from hitting the tree.

"I don't see nothing," I told him.

"It's higher up," he said.

I lifted his shirt a little more and revealed the hole in his back. There wasn't a lot of blood, but he was in a lot of pain. Seeing my brother with a hole in his back was the worst shit I'd ever seen. Not because someone was shot, but because it was my brother. I rushed back around to the driver's side and tried to start the car, but it wouldn't start. I asked him did he want me to call an ambulance or run for help because neither would be easy. He told me to run and get help. By this time, there nothing but vacant houses and fields on this particular street. The closest house I knew I could get help from was Hammer's house three blocks away. Completely terrified, I took off running as fast as I could. Those few minutes it took for me to get there were probably the worst minutes of my life.

I prayed to God that my brother didn't die while I was gone. I knew if he died, I'd never forgive myself. It was all my fault. I thought about what if I got here and Hammer wasn't at

KING BENJAMIN

home. I can't begin to describe the feelings that went through me as I prayed he was there.

"Please be home, please be home," was the only thought in my head.

I guess God was watching the whole thing play out because when I got there, Hammer was asleep on the couch right near the front door. I told him Black was shot and we needed to get him to a hospital right now. We jumped in his car and rushed back to the scene. When we got there, Black had crawled out of the car and was lying in the grass not moving. I walked up thinking he was dead, but when I called out his name, he responded. Hammer and I picked him up and put him in the back seat. Hammer ran every red light, doing about 80 miles an hour until we reached the hospital.

My brother was in extreme pain. We didn't know it then, but he'd been struck by an AK bullet. When we reached the hospital, as much as it pained me to leave, I knew I couldn't stay. The police would be showing up soon asking questions I knew I couldn't answer. Once we reached the hospital and he was still conscious, I knew in my heart he was going to make it. I was right. My brother would pull through. He was in really bad shape, but he survived. There was no doubt in my mind that God was with us both that night. This is a big part of the reason why I had to tell my story. I had to tell the world how God saved my life for a reason.

IS HE DEAD?

AFTER MY BROTHER HAD SURGERY, I went back to visit him in the hospital. In that short amount of time, he lost so much weight he looked like a starving child. His head was swollen to almost twice the normal size. I tried to be normal with him but seeing my brother in this condition was sending me into an uncontrollable rage all over again. My entire body was a blazing inferno. There was no way I could let this ride. There was no way this was going to be settled without more bloodshed. Face almost immediately called Hammer trying to clear his name, but I already knew Face wasn't the shooter. As I stated, Face wasn't built like that, but it was his truck so it might as well have been him behind the trigger.

It got back to me quickly that it was the dudes that were on the porch that night I shot at Face. It didn't make a difference to me who it was because I was planning to kill everyone affiliated with Face now. I hadn't seen or talked to Boogie, but just like my brother had my back, I had to assume he had his. Even in the middle of it all, the whole thought of killing one of my closest, if not my closest, friend just felt wrong. I'd always heard how the game and money could turn friends against each other. I was now a living example of that.

It didn't take me long to find out where Face was laying his head. I found out he'd broken up with his girl and was now laying up with some chick off Six Mile. I would creep through every night just waiting to catch him slipping going in or out. I wanted to empty a clip in his head so badly I could taste it, but

KING BENJAMIN

I had no such luck. Face had stopped going to the girl's house, realizing too many people knew about that spot. He'd shut the spot down and went into hiding the same night Black got shot. About a month went by before I would finally see him, or anybody affiliated with him again. I spotted his truck parked right in front of a friend's house. He was just sitting in his truck like everything was all good.

I crept up the block on foot slowly, hoping he wouldn't be aware of his surroundings. There weren't a lot of people outside. I saw a figure standing in the door at that house, so I pulled my hoodie over my head. I knew whoever it was could see me, which made me not want to get any closer, but I also didn't want to miss again either. I tried to get as close as I could, but my gut was telling me it wasn't the right time.

Someone was watching, standing in the doorway, but I couldn't let him get away because I didn't know how long it would be before I saw him again. From the sidewalk across the street, I pulled the drawstring tightly on my hoodie, took my gun out, and started dumping. I let off about six shots before I turned and ran through the field. Face's truck never moved, so I assumed he was dead.

I ran to my homey Chaz's house and told him what I'd just done. He grabbed the car keys and drove me out of the neighborhood lying down on the floor in the back of his car. Later on that evening, I got a call telling me that Face was wearing a vest and only had the wind knocked out of him. He was shaken up but otherwise okay. This news only fueled my thirst for blood.

The one good thing that came from my second attempt was that nobody from Face's camp would dare come to the hood for a while, so I was able to get back to hustling. Since I'd never officially left G-Block, I went right back and picked up where I'd left off. Black was still in the hospital and going through surgeries and learning how to digest food with a smaller stomach. That AK bullet had really torn up his insides

FIGHT OF MY LIFE

and it took him a long time to heal from all those surgeries. There was no one on the block but us. It seemed like the summer of 1996 was all about beef.

Around this same time, my homies that I grew up with, the same ones I ran with in high school, had beef with my connect. They had a plan to take over the hood. It didn't have anything to do with me so I didn't care, but they wanted Black and me to join them. Then my connect got shot but he survived. He called my brother in the hospital, asking him did we have anything to do with it. What he basically wanted to know was whose side were we on. I definitely didn't have anything to do with the shooting, but I did feel a sense of loyalty to the friends I grew up with. To keep my relationship with my connect, I just avoided everyone's calls for a while.

These guys I grew up with were watching my back while Black was in the hospital and had been looking out for me my whole life. These were the guys that were visiting my brother in the hospital, and they were the same guys that drove me out the hood in the back seat that day I thought I'd murdered Face. At the same time, even with all that, I could honestly say none of them had ever tried to help me get money up to that point, and the connect was trying to take me to the next level. I was conflicted to say the least. It was just a bad situation all the way around the board.

Then something else bad happened. Something no one was expecting. One night in June, three guys wearing ski masks knocked on Freaky's door. His girlfriend ran screaming.

"They at the door with masks on!" she panicked.

When Freaky ran to the door to see what was going on, the masked gunmen opened fired through the locked storm door, shooting him right in the chest. Freaky died in the ambulance on the way to the hospital. Nobody had a clue who had killed Freaky. Either way we looked at it didn't make sense. Freaky didn't even have beef, and he didn't have anything to do with the other beefs going on around him. He was the silly cat that smoked weed all day and tried to live in peace. His death shook everyone up including me. For a while, the whole hood was just in a dazed and confused state. There was so much gunplay and violence you never knew what would happen next. I think this was the time in my life that gave me PTSD, although I've never been officially diagnosed.

Eventually, Black came home with a tube still in his side. He wanted to go right back to hustling, but we made him stay in the house and heal up like he was supposed to. About a month after Freaky's death, I finally ran into the one person that could be a mediator in this ongoing beef I had. He was on the block hustling and using a crack head's house to cut up his dope. I often used the house for the same purpose, so this day we just happened to be there at the same time. When I saw him face to face, I saw no malice in his eyes. No anger or fear.

"Man, we need to talk," he said.

"You right, we do," I agreed.

This was the first time we'd seen each other since the night I shot at Face. Boogie spoke first. He went on to say that Face didn't want things to continue down this route and that I should've never gotten the guns involved. I explained to him that 225 versus 140 pounds wasn't a fair fight, but outside of that, there was another obvious point to be made. I explained everything that was said.

"When have you ever seen me let a nigga talk to me like that?" I questioned him.

"Still," was all he could say, shaking his head.

I also explained to him that had we fought and I lost, I would've came back with a gun anyway because this was where I eat.

"You know me, dog. How did you think this was gonna go? When have I ever let a nigga talk to me like that?" I repeated.

FIGHT OF MY LIFE

"You right," he agreed.

Just then, another fiend that worked for Boogie and Face at the time opened his mouth out of the blue.

"I should've killed you a long time ago."

I turned to make sure he was talking to me. He was.

"The only reason I ain't killed you is because I knew I would have to kill your brother and Jack too."

I asked him the same question I asked Face.

"Who the fuck do you think you talking to?"

"I'm talking to you, nigga!" he replied bravely.

I'll never know what made him speak to me this way, especially in the climate we were in and everything going on around us. I won't make it seem like this guy was a serious threat to me. He was crack head, but at the time, Face had given him a gun to protect the house he was hustling at. For that reason, and everything else leading up to that moment, I had to take him seriously this day.

I pulled my gun and marched up to him while he sat in a chair. My plan was to threaten his life and remind him who I was. I raised the gun and he reached for the barrel. He had a hand on the barrel just long enough to stand to his feet as three shots from the lemon squeeze trigger sounded. The barrel was aimed low as the gun went off. He fell to the floor. Everybody in the house took off out the front door. I looked at him lying on the floor bleeding. He was hurt badly. I walked out the front door and tucked the gun in my waist.

I walked through the dark streets to Don's old house, which his older sister lived in now. Even though I knew the guy was breathing when I left, something told me he was dying. The way he laid motionless on the ground didn't seem like a non-life-threatening injury. When I got to Don's sister's house, she showed me the bullet hole in my pants leg. Only then did I realize I'd shot myself in the process of the struggle. The bullet went in and out and I wasn't in pain.

KING BENJAMIN

I called the girl I was dating at the time to come and get me. When she picked me up, I told her I wanted to leave the city for a minute until I found out some information. She took me to her brother's house in Ann Arbor. I knew her brother and his wife and I was comfortable there. The next morning, I got the call from my mother and a bunch of other people telling me that the guy I shot was dead.

Before he passed, he managed to give police my nickname. The guy who lived in the house told police where to find me. They raided the spot that same night and got Jack and his uncle. Under pressure, one of the two gave up my real identity and the rest of the information police would need to find me if I was still in Detroit. The police went to my mother's house and everywhere else I hung out. That's how my mom found out about it. I could only imagine what it was like for her when they knocked on her door and told her that I was wanted for questioning in a homicide.

That's when I realized how fucked up my life had become. All the anger and resentment towards my enemies meant nothing. All the plotting and creeping around trying to hit Face seemed pointless now. I had killed a man that wasn't even involved in the war. Now I was on the run and it was the worst feeling in the world. My head was all over the place, but I knew it wasn't the time to crack under pressure. I had to pull myself together and figure out my next move.

The next day, I called home and told my mother I needed to get out of state. I knew the only people that would take me in under these types of circumstances was family. She tried to talk me into dealing with the situation head on instead of running. I disagreed immensely with that approach. I was twenty years old with my whole life ahead of me. To turn myself in to police sounded insane at the time. I couldn't think of one good reason to go and talk to police so they could lock me in a cell and throw away the key. How was I going to

FIGHT OF MY LIFE

convince them I didn't do something that at least three other people saw me do? I had to run.

The next day, I got a call saying I needed to leave Ann Arbor immediately. Jack's girlfriend, who was also a cousin to the girl I was with, had gone to the police station and told them where I was. She'd hung me out to dry hoping they would let him go, but he was still locked up because he had warrants of his own. We left her brother's house immediately and checked into a nearby hotel. Thirty minutes after we left, the police raided the townhouse with ten cars. We found out because she'd mistakenly called her brother's wife while police were still inside the house. I told her don't call anybody else.

Before police left the house, they posted wanted pictures with my face all around the area on telephone poles. I knew Ann Arbor wasn't safe for me. I had my lady friend call the train and the Greyhound bus station to see what was leaving first. I remember drinking a half pint of Hennessy in just the short time it took her to make the calls. I was thinking I wouldn't make it out of Ann Arbor. When she got off the phone, she said, "You sure is calm to be on the run."

I guess she didn't see me dust off the half pint of liquor to calm my nerves. As I sat there, I realized that we'd called her brother's house from the hotel phone. If the police were on their job, they might check the caller ID and put it together that it was us calling. I couldn't take that chance. So after only being at the Comfort Inn about an hour, we went right across the street and checked in at the Days Inn. By then, we had already found out what time the bus was leaving. We called the cab and it arrived twenty minutes later.

I paid for two hotel rooms in an hour and a half and I wouldn't need either one of them. I remember I was the most anxious at the moment I got in the cab. I kept thinking about if police came into the hotel parking lot the cab driver would probably lock me inside. By now, my mom had called my uncle in St. Louis and told him I was coming. I just needed to stay with him for a week or two until I could figure some things out. When I got to the Greyhound bus station, I gave the girl two thousand dollars. I told her to try and find a house outside of Detroit. I knew I would want to come back to Michigan one day and I needed to have a safe haven.

In the bus station, I sat there on the curb, not knowing if the police were on my escape route already. I scooted next to some white girl so it would look like we were together. I figured if the police came, they would probably be looking for me and the girl I was with. I struck up a conversation with the white girl and tried to act normal.

Although police had my picture, they didn't have any mugshots of me because I didn't have any real priors. About five minutes after I sat next to the girl, the police showed up. I lowered my head and continued to converse with the girl, trying to act normal. I couldn't believe it when they walked right past me and up onto the bus that was about to pull off. I'll never know if they were actually there looking for me or not, but the timing of it sure as hell felt like it. About five minutes after the police left, my bus to Missouri showed up. I'd never been so happy to see a bus in my life.

****

In St. Louis, I got a chance to see a lot of my family members, some of whom I'd never even met. My uncle was a recovering drug addict, and everything smelled like crack to him. When I used the spray deodorant I'd packed in my luggage, he'd come to the bathroom door and say, "What's that smell? Something stinks. Smells like dope. If you smoking dope, you gotta leave."

He did the same thing when I used the antiseptic I'd bought to keep the wound in my leg clean. It was very obvious

FIGHT OF MY LIFE

I wasn't going to be there long. I just tried to get my mind together and enjoy the city for the time being. The more time I had to think, the more my common sense kicked in. At first, I thought I might've been able to set up shop and get my hustle on in St. Louis.

But once I realized my uncle was no longer connected to the streets, that ruined everything. The rest of my family were regular working-class people with no street ties. I realized if I stayed in Missouri, I'd be broke in no time. I'd spent three thousand dollars the first week of being on the run. I decided to talk to a lawyer about the specifics of what I was charged with. To my surprise, the lawyer all but promised me that if I turned myself in, he could get me five years or less. This was the first indication that my life might not be over.

I had a decision to make. Should I hire a lawyer while I still had the money to do so, or should I just play catch me if you can and worry about that day when it came? I knew I didn't want to spend the rest of my life on the run. It was a horrible feeling. After being on the run for less than two weeks, I came back to Detroit and went into the lawyer's office. He immediately called the homicide division and made arrangements for me to turn myself in. The crazy part was, after all the searching and raiding houses, the homicide detective working the case went on vacation.

They literally told the lawyer it wouldn't make sense for me to turn myself in until the detective got back because I'd just sit in the police headquarters waiting for his return. I couldn't believe it, but that was the second indication that my situation might not be as bad as it seemed. I was back in Detroit but technically still on the run. I went to see the women in my life to get some last-minute sex before the day came for me to turn myself in.

I went to the hood to holler at my homies. Most of them agreed that I was doing the right thing by retaining a lawyer and turning myself in. The more I thought about it, I started

KING BENJAMIN

to believe the case wasn't that strong, otherwise I'd be locked in a cell somewhere already. About a week went by and I made arrangements to turn myself in on July 24, 1996, four days before my 21st birthday.

That morning, I smoked a blunt before I had my lady friend drive me downtown. When I walked in and told them what I was there for, they were very nonchalant about it all. They made me sit and wait on a bench near the front door as if they didn't care if I stayed or left. I thought about leaving the entire time I was sitting in that lobby. After about twenty-five minutes, someone finally came and led me to a small interrogation room. Soon after, they started the whole good cop, bad cop thing.

One was supposed to be on my side while the other would come in when he left and tell me how much trouble I was in and how much time I was about to do. I gave them both my name and refused to answer any questions without my lawyer present. The put me in a holding cell where I would remain for days. I immediately began to reflect on all the good and the bad I'd experienced in the game. Then I started crunching numbers to see just how old I'd be when I got home if I got the kind of time the bad cop said I was facing.

According to him, I'd be at least 41 years old when I got out. This was the first time I really started to evaluate how I ended up in this predicament. I felt like I was really just playing the cards I was dealt. Knowing what was ahead of me if I didn't try to make my situation better, I chose the illegal route. I'd found a way to be someone I was proud of at the time and help my family with their financial situation. But in the end, look where it had landed me.

People always say you make choices to do right or wrong. Sometimes you don't see those clear choices when you're surrounded by so much negativity in the hood. When I made those choices, they felt like the only option. Sometimes all you can see is opportunity when it knocks and you're afraid if you

FIGHT OF MY LIFE

don't take it, it may never knock again. So the choice feels like shit or get off the pot instead of right and wrong. At least that's what it felt like to me.

Knowing there was only one way that I could dig myself out of this, I did what everyone does at their lowest. I talked to God for the next few days, and I told Him that I knew I was going to have to make some changes and that I needed His help if that was going to happen. As a child, my faith in God was strong, but growing up in the hood made me feel like I couldn't realistically maintain a relationship with God. I was doing too much dirt to stay close to Him. Still, once I was in deep shit, I found myself calling on Him. I prayed every night for the best possible outcome in court. I promised to stop carrying guns as part of my commitment to change. I'd never prayed harder in my life than I did in those four days.

I went to court on my 21st birthday and in what seemed like a miraculous turn of events, I received a personal bond on a second-degree murder charge, which meant I didn't have to pay a dime to make bail. I knew then that I'd made the right decision in turning myself in. That day taught me the power of a good lawyer but more importantly, the power of prayer. I knew someone had to be listening. I was headed back to the streets after all the running and hiding. I was so extremely happy and grateful for the blessing I'd just received, but sadly enough, it wasn't long before I was back up to my old tricks.

OUT ON BOND

WHEN I GOT OUT OF JAIL, everyone thought I was still on the run. I came through the hood and people were acting like they'd just seen a ghost. I told them the truth about being out on a personal bond, but some people still didn't believe me. Hustling had been my only form of income and it was all I knew. It was less than a week of sitting still before I knew I had to get back to work. The block was banging like never before. I knew regardless of all the praying I did, I wasn't ready to give up the way I made my money.

When I got back to the block, I realized there was a lot going on. We had two houses now instead of one. G-Block was getting drugs from two different connects that just happened to be beefing with each other at the time. It was a train wreck waiting to happen. My old plug, and a family member of a guy I grew up with, were both supplying the spots. Eventually, Deuce, the family member, found out about it and he got upset and burned one of the houses down that we hustled in while they still owed him a bunch of money.

When he did this, of course everybody from G-Block that owed him money kept the money and the drugs, which caused even more tension between all of us. It was the last thing I needed. I didn't owe him anything, but I still wanted to retaliate on principle. I was still of the opinion that Deuce had violated by burning down one of our drug houses. Even though I had left G-Block briefly, I would always have access to that income because it was me that started the whole operation in the first

FIGHT OF MY LIFE

place. The agreement was that each of us would always be entitled to a percentage of the money that was made on that block.

This was why I took it so personal that the house was burned down. It was just as disrespectful as a kick-door robbery. Regardless of what I promised God, I was ready for war, but Black had the clearer head at the time. He'd been through a lot already and now that he didn't have to pay Deuce, things were going pretty good for him. He had money of his own, plus he'd just made a quick come up. He told me the last thing I needed was to catch another case on top of the one I was facing. Besides that, we still had the other house, so it wasn't slowing down our momentum at all.

After I agreed not to strike back, some time passed without incident and I began to feel the same way Black did, but to this day, it still bothers me that we didn't do shit about Deuce burning up that house. With all the beef going on, it wasn't long before shit got hot and things slowed way down. Black saw an opportunity to branch out and we ended up venturing out into another hood.

My brother and I set up shop on Six Mile and Davison. We still had money coming from G-Block, but it wasn't enough. Not too long after that, Face popped back up in the hood trying to hustle, thinking we were gone. We started to creep through the hood to see if we could catch him sticking his neck out. I knew we would never get the dude that actually shot up my car, because they weren't even from the city and hadn't been back since. Black had a serious vendetta after all he'd been through, and I knew eventually one of us would catch up with Face.

One night, Face was gunned down in the driveway of his old crack house, but he survived his injuries. Not too long after that, he and his brother were arrested on unrelated murder charges. Eventually, they would both beat the charges, but all the trials and tribulations would lead to Face waving the white

KING BENJAMIN

flag and retiring from the game. Looking back on it all, I don't blame him.

I continued to hustle in the new hood with Black as the old block became just about a ghost town. One day, we had a sit-down with the guys that were responsible for burning the house down. *Why would we have a sit-down with these guys?* Because with the exception of Deuce, these were the same guys we'd grown up with and ran with all our lives. Some of these guys were right there scrapping back-to-back with us in high school. We all had love for each other until the game got ahold of us.

When we had the sit-down, everyone in the room was strapped and the tension was thick. I had a seventeen-shot nine and my brother had a Mac-11. I let Black do the talking because it was initially his beef. On the surface, everyone's anger had supposedly faded away with time, but we all knew the tension was still very real. When discussions started, it was mostly about two major violations. The house that was burnt down and the money that was taken in retaliation. Giving the money back wasn't an option, so it left us at a sort of a standstill.

They couldn't put the house back, so he wasn't giving up any money. In the end, it was all about principles and respect. Since nobody was harmed, we were all able to walk away from the situation with our lives and eventually our friendships intact.

On my first court appearance, the new judge had snatched my personal bond and took me off the streets momentarily. She thought it was ridiculous that I was on a personal bond after being charged with such a serious crime. She gave me a ten-thousand-dollar bond with ten percent due, which meant I only had to pay a thousand dollars. I was out that same day, but it made me glad I had gone right back to hustling.

The new spot we had began to really pick up eventually, but it seemed like every time I made some money, I was paying my lawyer, helping someone with bills, or taking a loss. I

FIGHT OF MY LIFE

reinvested all my profits back into drugs to stay above water. This went on for months. Every time I would get a court date, my lawyer would push the next date further and further away, giving me as much time as he could on the streets. The chances of me beating the case were slim, but I was convinced I wouldn't have to do time for second-degree murder.

There were a lot of surrounding facts that I won't get into, but I knew if I went to trial, they would never get that to stick. After eight months of stalling, I finally had to face the music. They prosecutor offered me a plea of involuntary manslaughter. Outside of beating the charges completely, it was the best deal I could hope for. At the end of the day, I realized a life was lost and I was responsible for it, but I also realized that once he grabbed the gun, it could've easily been me. I took the plea and the judge set a date for me to come back and get sentenced.

During the month I was waiting to get sentenced, I continued to hustle all the way up until the day before it was time to go to jail. I also tried to spend time with the people I cared about and prepare myself mentally for whatever the next chapter of my life was about to bring. Coming from the life I was living, I always knew that prison came with the territory. Once it was my time, I still hated to know that when I woke up that morning, it would be a long time before I saw the streets again. In court, the judge sentenced me to four to fifteen years. Just like that, my whole life was on pause, and the bailiff took me away in cuffs. Once I was placed in that tiny cell all alone, I remember it feeling like the end of the world for about five minutes. After that, I was ready for the journey.

PRISON LIFE

I SAT IN THE COUNTY jail about six days waiting to go to prison. The county jail felt like the worst place in the world to be. Packed in with the lowest forms of life that the city had to offer, I'd be lying if I said I didn't feel uncomfortable and out of place. Seemed like hardly anybody showered or brushed their teeth. Not only that, you'd meet some of dumbest criminals in America in the county jail. I never thought I'd be so happy to go to prison but when it was my time to go, I was overjoyed just to get out of the county.

After the county, I went to Jackson quarantine for a month while the system figured out who had bed space for me. One of the most degrading experiences is when you first get to quarantine, you have to strip naked and open your ass cheeks so they know you're not sneaking something in the prison.

That's also gotta be the worst job in the world for a straight man to have to do on a daily basis. Just looking at buttholes all damn day. That whole experience alone probably turned some dudes away from a life of crime for good. From Jackson, I was sent to a level-two prison called Newberry. Newberry was a real prison, but it didn't look like one to me. It looked like a college campus. It was clean, it had cubicles that reminded me of dorms, and a bunch of extracurricular things to keep you busy. Even though it had all of this stuff, an inmate could easily die in Newberry Correctional Facility.

There were twelve to sixteen people in each cubicle. There were a lot of young dudes my age, a lot of lifers, and a lot of gay boys. When I arrived there, cigarettes were still illegal to

FIGHT OF MY LIFE

possess, so most of the violence that went down was because of cigarettes. If you were lucky enough to sneak cigarettes in, you had to be built to last because you immediately became a target. Dudes were getting their heads busted or stabbed so much behind Bugler cigarettes, they eventually allowed the prison to have them and started to sell them in the store.

I had a lot of friends from Van Dyke at Newberry with me. To be honest, the first few months was like a big family reunion. I mean, these were some wild and crazy dudes, so once people realized how many of us were on the compound, we just didn't have any problems unless one of us created some. I did realize that if I wasn't careful, I could end up in prison for fifteen years instead of four, so I tried to be smart about how I moved. My Van Dyke homies had a lot of bad habits and they didn't take prison that seriously.

They got weed from people and didn't pay. They borrowed money from people and didn't pay. Some of them even squeezed small-town dudes for money. There was one guy I was friends with named Pete. He was a friend of a friend, but he was around all the time. He joined a religious group and worked his way up in the ranking just for the purpose of abusing his power. He had no interest in the religion whatsoever. It was good to have him on our side though, because it kept down a lot of conflict between us and the religious groups.

At first, I played the prison yard all day every day, but as time went on, I realized I could be using it more wisely. I wanted to accomplish some things while I was behind bars. The first thing on my list was to finish school. I knew it would make my mom proud and one day when I had a kid, I could tell them to finish school with a straight face. It also looks good to the parole board if they saw you didn't spend all the time learning to be a better criminal.

I took the GED test and passed the first time with really high-test scores. It felt so invigorating to accomplish something positive. I knew right then I wanted to experience that feeling of accomplishment as many times as I could in life. I started setting small goals for myself. I wanted to read at least thirty books before I went home. At the time, I probably hadn't read and finished 30 books my whole life. I also decided I wanted to gain some weight while I was in jail, so I set a goal to put on twenty pounds.

Those were the things I started to spend my days doing. If I wasn't in the weight room, I was in my cubicle reading and writing raps. I kicked it with my homeboys less and less because I had a schedule to keep me busy. At that point, I still had a small urge to become a rapper so while I had time, I started working on an album. The time started flying by and before I knew it, I had a rap album completed, I was twenty pounds heavier, and had read about fifteen books. That was the point when I started to feel like I could do whatever I set my mind to. I mean, as long as I was working towards a goal, I would look up and I'd accomplished it.

But in my mind, I was still only training to become a better criminal. I'd sold drugs all the way up to my sentencing day and had plans to sell as soon as I got out again. When I went on the yard, I was getting game from my OGs about how to last in the dope game. I got game from the goons on how to set niggas up, kidnap niggas, you name it. These dudes literally robbed and stole for a living and they had a million ways to do it. They had no conscience or remorse. They weren't good people that somehow made one mistake and landed in jail. They were Satan's angels.

I'd already had a get rich or die trying mentality but after spending enough time with these guys, I knew if my hustle hand ever fell off, I would always have a plan B tucked away. I was in prison when I learned how to smuggle drugs in and out of state, how to cook crack, and even how to fake my own death if I needed to. Newberry was definitely a class for criminals if nothing else.

FIGHT OF MY LIFE

After a year and a half, my level dropped and I went to a camp. As soon as I got to camp, I realized that it was nothing like a real prison. If anyone has ever gone to jail and done all their time in a camp or a minimum-security prison, they can't really testify as to what prison life is like. I mean, you still miss your family and freedom, but camp was more like a vacation than anything. At Newberry, you could come out of the unit and see a trail of blood in the hallway any time after an inmate got poked. At camp, everyone was just trying to go home. All the way up north, I was surrounded by beautiful nature, I had my own room all to myself, and we even had cable television, and a salad bar that they brought out with every dinner.

The food wasn't bad at all, but I thought it was a joke when I heard about the salad bar. I mean, in Newberry the food was straight garbage and you had to constantly watch your back. In camp niggas were friendly and carried themselves in a way more relaxed manner. There was no one doing life. No one even doing five years. It was the most peaceful time I ever did.

At camp I was really able to get my mind right and focus on my plans for the future. I felt like I was still really young and had a lot of hustle in me. I planned to come home and stack up a hundred thousand and start investing my money. I thought about all the things that held my interest, real estate, clothing, and music. I knew I could make money off something besides selling dope, but I was stuck on the old adage it takes money to make money. I started talking completely different than I did before I came to prison.

I was about twenty-three at the time and everything was money and power moves. I wasn't getting high or drinking, so I saw everything clearly and rationally. I realized my ambitions were high and that I needed to prepare myself mentally for all the labor that was ahead. I also realized how much I wanted to get out of the hood one day. I developed a belief system that basically hard work pays off no matter what you're doing. Legal or illegal, right or wrong. If you work hard, you will succeed…or so I thought.

My last stop on this jail journey was a camp closer to home. I ran into my man Kev from Van Dyke. Kev was a hustler who had gotten caught with a half a kilo and sentenced to ten years. When I linked up with him, he was almost a year away from seeing the parole board. Kev had some rich niggas waiting on him to come home, but he told me he wasn't going back to selling coke. If anything, he'd push some weed and try to reach his goals with that.

Kev became my workout partner and we kicked it every day. All we talked about was the future. We'd both been lucky to make it to camp after all the dirt we'd been involved in while in prison. Physically and mentally, I was in the best shape of my life. I'd have to say the time I spent in those facilities back then turned out to be more of a good thing than bad. If I'd stayed on the streets, I would've probably been dead but now I was older, smarter, and had way more focus.

When I put my papers in to go to the halfway house, I got immediately approved. I exchanged phone numbers with Kev and about five other people that I planned to keep in contact with. I had to go back to Jackson for another thirty days while I waited on bed space at the halfway house. Because of good time, I had a few months knocked off my sentence.

I was ready for the streets. Three years and one month after I was sentenced, I was headed back to Detroit. I remember thinking to myself that prison life wasn't as rough as I thought it would be. Looking back on it now, I feel like I set myself up by taking it so lightly.

WTF?

WHEN I CAME BACK TO Detroit to start my stay at the halfway house, my self-esteem was higher than I'd ever experienced. I mean, really through the roof. I'd learned so much about myself while away and I believed in myself more than I ever did before. I felt like it was truly my time. The week my plug caught beef, he'd offered to front me a whole kilo if I paid for half up front. After the beef jumped off, he became unavailable. The week I caught my case, I was a couple thousand short of copping my first kilo anyway. Then Boogie offered to go half in with me. I was right there at the doorstep of the success I wanted. Then all hell broke loose.

This time, I felt like there was no stopping me. I didn't have a lot of hangouts or bad habits that would keep me from being successful. I didn't gamble, I didn't trick, and because of parole, I wouldn't even smoke weed. As far as I could see, I was destined for success and the world was mine for the taking.

We arrived at the placement around noon. I didn't know any of the dudes I came with, so I kept to myself. I knew the halfway house held men and women, so I was interested in seeing what kind of thug chicks were roaming through the joint. It wasn't long before I realize it was mostly crackheads and prostitutes residing there. First thing we did was go to orientation. I knew about the zero-tolerance policy that basically meant if we screwed up in any way, we would go straight back to prison. What I didn't know was that they would have a straight-up Nazi running the whole operation.

KING BENJAMIN

This man who was in charge of my freedom had no respect for felons and felt it was his job to make things as hard as he possibly could. His words were more than harsh, and he talked like it was his job to dehumanize and humiliate us. If I didn't know any better, I would've thought they made a wrong turn and dropped us off at boot camp. He basically told us he was there to make our lives miserable and he hoped that we just gave up and went on the run instead of trying to tough it out. A lot of people took him up on that offer.

It was easy to escape from there. All you had to do was hang out in the lobby like you were waiting to use the phone and soon as the doors opened, you break wide. No one was going to chase you, so once you made it outside you were free. Some people ran out the first day. I didn't get it though. *How did they think coming straight home and going back on the run was a good idea?* I had to try and make this thing work for all the people that held me down and were waiting for me to come home.

At that point, I'd only had one real serious relationship, and even though we weren't together anymore, Lisa held me down while I was gone. I called her and told her I wanted her to meet me at my mom's house once I started getting home visits. The first week we had to stay inside and after that, we were supposed to go out and start job searching through the week, and you got to go home and visit your family on the weekends. My first Saturday home visit, my boy Hammer came to pick me up and take me shopping. It was May of 2000 and the sun was shining brightly, setting the mood for a great day. Black Rob's "Woah" had just dropped, and I remember us riding to the mall playing it over and over.

When I got to the mall, that's when I truly felt alive again. Being surrounded by beautiful women and shopping to get fresh were the two things I needed to feel like myself again. I didn't waste any time getting at women in the mall either. I was on everything that looked up to my standards, and my standards were high as hell. Like I said, my confidence had

FIGHT OF MY LIFE

skyrocketed and the girls I came in contact with could sense that confidence. I remember I bagged the chick that was standing in Macy's with the sample cologne, waiting to spray you when you walked by. I was really looking forward to kicking it with her.

After we left the mall, we went to the hood and visited a lot of my homeboys I hadn't seen since I got locked up. It was amazing how in three years, nothing in the hood had changed. Most people were doing the exact same as when I left. There were a select few that had changed their financial status for better and some for worse. But for the most part, everything was the same. I only had about five hours for my home visit and I didn't want to chance being late, so I went back early. The next day was Mother's Day and I planned to spend that with my mom.

Even though it was Mother's Day, I still hadn't had sex yet and that was at the very top of my agenda too. I invited Lisa over to spend the day with us. I knew my mom would just be glad to have one of her sons home on this day. My brother was locked up on drug charges he'd caught on our old block years earlier. The day started out beautifully. I had a chance to enjoy the two most important women in my life, and I was feeling like a million bucks after Lisa and I snuck upstairs and had sex quicker than I even thought was possible.

When it was time for me to go back, I tried to leave early again just to be on the safe side. Lisa was having car trouble so even though she'd driven the car over there to see me, I didn't want her risking driving it further than she needed to. Instead of her dropping me off at the halfway house the way we planned, I told her to take the car home and park it. I'd just jump in a cab and head back. My stepdad didn't have a car at the time, so that was my best option. After she left, I called a cab and then another one. Getting a cab at my mom's house was never a problem because when I wasn't driving, I took a cab everywhere. On top of that, my mom lived on a nice quiet

KING BENJAMIN

block now, so danger was never a factor to consider for cab drivers.

This particular day, I called cab after cab and no one showed up. Time wasn't on my side any longer, so I walked up to the main street to flag one down. That didn't work either. All of sudden, I looked up and I had about twenty minutes to make it back or I'd be violated. I ran and knocked on my neighbor's door. I told him I'd pay him whatever he needed to take me back, but we had to leave right now. Only problem was that my neighbor was older and he naturally moved at a slower pace than I would've under the circumstances.

It took him ten minutes to get ready to leave. Once he did get ready and we finally left the house, he was driving at a turtle's pace, which only added to my anxiety. At the speed he was driving, it would take us at least thirty minutes to get there. I asked if he could speed it up so I could make it on time, and he basically cursed me out and told me he wasn't catching a speeding ticket for no muthafucka. The whole ride there, I was thinking if I was only a few minutes late maybe someone would show me a little mercy and let me stay there with a warning. But now I was already a few minutes late and far away from my destination. The closer we got, I kept hearing the Nazi's voice in my head telling me how I'd go straight back to prison if I was even one minute late.

As fear began to consume me, I started to weigh my options. I'd been out two weeks. It didn't take long for me to realize I wasn't prepared to go right back to prison. I told the old man to pull over at the next gas station. There was no way I could get out of prison and return in the same month. I'd seen guys do it before and they were the laughingstock of the compound when they returned. I found a cab easily once I wasn't in dire need of one. Instead of going to my mom's house, I went straight to the hood. I couldn't go back to my mom's house. They'd be looking for me there.

FIGHT OF MY LIFE

Hammer tried to talk me out of going on the run, but I had made a choice and that was that. Once he realized there was no talking me out of it, he had my back to the fullest. He gave me his bachelor pad to chill at while he shacked up with one of his girlfriends. By now, Sal had come home from prison also and was working in a factory. When I gave Sal the bad news, he just kept saying 'What the fuck? How the hell did that happen?' I was thinking that same exact thing. *How did I go from prison to on the run in two weeks?* I could've just run out of the door the first day like the rest of them. The hardest part of it all was when I had to tell my mom. That was a tough conversation and she cried the entire time.

All the confidence in myself and my plans for the future were completely shattered. I got drunk and high as I could to keep from thinking about the situation. I passed out at the bachelor pad that night just knowing I was utterly screwed. I didn't know what I was going to do with myself from there. The next day, I tried to get organized the best I could. Hammer came through and gave me a half pound of weed just to keep some money in my pocket. That way, at least I didn't have to worry about how I was going to feed myself. That's when I learned just how slow the weed game could be if you weren't already established in it.

That same day, I went out to hustle the weed and I quickly realized everybody was selling weed now. It didn't even matter if you had good weed or not because everybody knew where to find some good weed. There was no point in them risking buying bullshit weed from me. I didn't have the patience to build a strong weed clientele so as soon as I sold it all, I bought some crack. I didn't have a spot and I couldn't be out on the stroll because I was a wanted man.

I asked Hammer could I let a few of my big spenders come to the weed house. He okayed it at first and things were going smoothly. Then the crackheads started being crackheads and doing things that couldn't be tolerated. They'd pull up in broad daylight with a car full of white boys, making it look like an all-out crack house. I couldn't even be mad when Hammer said I couldn't do it anymore. He had a low-key spot with a real nice flow going, and the last thing he needed was that kind of heat.

Hammer was doing all he could to help me. He'd given me a place to stay and a means to hustle, so I had to stand on my own from there. I started working by pager only, which slowed business way down. Fiends didn't have the patience for it. I knew I had to do something fast, or I'd be broke with no money and no product to sell. The next time I went to re-up, I bought some powdered coke and had my boy stretch two ounces into three. This turned out to be a bad decision as well. While I was gone, the whip game had all but disappeared, so my bad dope stuck out like a sore thumb.

Not to mention that I was still working from a pager. Who was going to page me to bring them the worst dope they could find? It took me forever to sell that package. I had to steal other niggas' customers like Feezy used to do to us on that one block. This forced me to carry a pistol everywhere I went because I knew if someone caught me serving in front of their spot, it was going down. By the time I finished the package, I had very little money. Even when I got some better dope my reputation was already ruined. I realized it wouldn't be long before I either caught a dope case or some major beef behind violating other niggas' businesses. For the second time in my life, I had to fall back from hustling. But that only left me with a huge question mark. What do I do now?

NO WOMEN, NO KIDS

I SAT AROUND THE HOUSE for a while, getting high and listening to music, feeling discredited as a hustler. I had met this little, short, chocolate girl with a really nice figure that I'd been having sex with to kill time. I definitely wasn't in my right mind at this time, and I made a critical mistake. I hit it once without a condom and she gave me trichomonas. The worst part was I turned around and gave it to Lisa. She cursed me out, telling me I could've given her AIDs, and she was right. After that, she stopped dealing with me and I stopped dealing with Chocolate, so now I had nobody. I was also flat broke, and I knew the chances were slim of meeting somebody new in the foreseeable future just sitting in the house all day.

I grew more miserable by the day. Hammer usually would stop by every few days to check on me. One day he just stopped coming by, and so did everyone else. By the end of the week, there was no food in the house to eat, and mentally, I was going off the deep end. I feel my depression rising to an all-time high. My cell phone was off so I couldn't call anyone. I just waited ... and waited. Completely out of everything to eat but bread, I began to feel a form of desperation I'd never known before. The kind you can feel all in your veins.

I searched the house from top to bottom looking for enough weed to just roll up a joint and ease my mind. Hammer was the weed man, so I just knew if I looked long enough I'd find some discarded buds lying around. I searched all the corners, cracks, and crevices you might drop some weed while

KING BENJAMIN

bagging up, until I eventually found some weed under the couch. It was just enough for a whole blunt.

I can admit, I felt like a crackhead practically ransacking the house just to find enough weed to smoke, but I needed something to keep my mind from spinning more out of control than it already was. After I smoked, it only made my hunger pains worse. Looking back on it, besides the day my brother was shot, this had to be the single worst day of my life. I knew nothing about the mind and how it worked and because I didn't understand how your pride could kill you, I went the entire day without eating a thing.

All I had to do was get out of the house, find my way to payphone, or any phone, and call someone, but that thought never occurred to me. I was locked into the moment of reality, knowing that everything had failed and there was no one to blame. I probably got about four hours of sleep that night, but it was enough to snap back into reality.

The next day, I went to the phone both and made a collect call to Sal. In the next hour or so, he was pulling up to the apartment. I explained to him that my situation was dire, and I couldn't sit back and wait on Hammer to do me any more favors. We started discussing my options. Sal told me he knew somebody we could rob for a few pounds of weed. It didn't take any convincing for me to agree to it. I was literally starving and looking for a way to change my situation immediately. I'd learned more about how to rob in prison than I'd ever known. It was time to put that knowledge to work. We rode around waiting for nightfall. Once it was dark, we rode to the guy we called Jeremy's house. I knew Jeremy and as far as I was concerned, he was soft, so this would be easy. I was about to take everything he had.

Sal parked down the street so it would appear that I was alone and just happened to be in the neighborhood. When Jeremy let me in, I told him I had a chick that lived right around the corner. I asked him if he had some weed and he said yes.

FIGHT OF MY LIFE

No sooner than he said it, his kids came running down the steps. I was already in a zone and ready to make a move, but now I was just stumped.

Then his girl came down the stairs and spoke to me. I was so desperate it never crossed my mind that he lived with his girl and his kids, plus Sal never brought it up. There was no way I was pulling a gun on him in front of his girl or kids, but I couldn't leave emptyhanded either. Hunger and mental breakdown were waiting for me back at that the apartment. Something had to give in order for me to feel like a man again. I could feel my anxiety rising while I sat there watching the game and making small talk. I asked about the price for a few pounds, and he gave me a price but told me he'd have to make a call for it. The plan just kept going downhill the longer I sat there.

At that point, I should've just got up and left, but all I could think about was the night before when I almost drove myself crazy thinking of how to get out of this black hole. I asked to see the weed and he sent the kids upstairs. Shortly after, his girlfriend followed the kids upstairs. He showed me the weed and that shit looked like dark brown hay. I was so mad I wanted to shoot him just on the strength of him trying to sell me that garbage. But as I held the weed in my hands, I realized it was this or nothing. If the kids and/or the girl came back downstairs, I'd leave emptyhanded. I could give him the weed back or I could take it and leave.

I glanced at the chain around his neck and that was all the extra motivation I needed to go for it. I pulled the pistol and told him to take off the chain. The look of total disbelief was all in his eyes. I tried to rob him quickly and quietly as possible. The whole time, he was looking at me like I was an animal and to be honest, I felt like one. I took the jewelry and the weed and ran off into the night. As Sal and I were riding home discussing the details of the incident, his cellphone rang. It's his mother on the phone. His mother wanted him to tell me to call my mother. I quickly called my mother.

KING BENJAMIN

"Hello?" she answered. "Son, I just got a call saying you robbed somebody. Please tell me that's not true."

I couldn't believe it. I tried to deny it, but mothers always have a way of knowing when their kids are lying. I found out later that his girlfriend, whose sister was a friend of the family, had made the call to rat me out. Every sign and symbol that this was a bad idea was there and I still went through with it. I hated myself for being so stupid, for stooping so low. To this day, it bothers me that I broke my mom's heart like that. I had to find a way to make it up to her.

MAMA NEEDS ME

THE JEWELRY I ROBBED JEREMY for wasn't worth much, and the weed was worth even less. If I add on the humiliation I caused my mother, that robbery was without a doubt the worst decision I'd ever made in my life. About a month later, Jeremy pulled up on me while I was walking back from Coney Island and shot at me a couple times. He wasn't as soft as I thought. I went looking for him a few days later, only to find out he'd moved.

Nothing was going my way in the streets, and my mother stayed crying because she was struggling as well. My dad had gotten laid off again from his job, and there just wasn't enough coming in to pay the bills. He also started to drink heavily around this time. I realized if I went back to jail at that moment, I'd leave my parents in a fucked up situation. There was no one to help them out but me, and I didn't have a dime. Nothing was making sense and all I could think about was helping my mom.

I did the only reasonable thing I could think of at the time. I moved back in with my mom and started looking for a job through the temp services in the area. The first job was $34 a day. I was slaving in a hot factory for three days and then they stopped calling us in. The next job I found was a lot better. It paid $7.50 an hour and there was lots of overtime. The job was building U-Haul trucks in Novi, Michigan. I had to get up at 4:30 in the morning and catch two buses to the temp service and then board the temp service bus to Novi.

KING BENJAMIN

After a month, I got a dollar raise. The bus rides there and back were so long I never had time to do anything but go to work and come home. I was never late, and I never missed a day. I wasn't happy at all, but I knew I was making my mother proud and helping her out tremendously. After that robbery thing, I felt like I owed this to her. I got paid every week and each check, I'd keep enough money for a haircut and bus fare, giving her the rest for bills. The job as a whole was cool, but the lifestyle was lackluster, to say the least. After a few months, all of my parents' bills were caught up. I still didn't have anything, but I felt like I was being a responsible adult, and that boosted myself esteem a little. I felt like a man again.

As my mom found a better job, my seasonal position came to an end. It was right before Christmas so people at the job were in a panic, but I didn't care. As long as my mom was cool, I was good. The temp service we worked for didn't offer me another job, so I was basically shit out of luck. I looked at a few more temp services but when nothing panned out, I decided it was time to get back to what I knew best. I got a call from Sal saying the police had been to his house looking for me. I had to get ID to get a job, and my ID had his address as my residence.

I knew it was just a matter of time before they came to my mother's house looking for me. I knew it was only God's will that I'd gotten away with living there that long. I called my homebody Chaz and told him I wanted to make a trip out of town ASAP. He told me he was leaving out Saturday and I could ride with him. I thought if I could just make it to Saturday morning, I'd be cool.

I could shoot out of town, make some quick money, and think of a plan from there. When Saturday morning came, I was all packed and ready to go. I got this strong feeling in my gut that I needed to leave my mother's house immediately. I had too much luggage to leave walking. By now, Lisa had forgiven me and we were back friends again. I told her to come

FIGHT OF MY LIFE

get me and I'd just have Chaz pick me up from her house. About fifteen minutes later, the doorbell rang.

I headed down the stairs, thinking it's Lisa. My mom told me the police were at the door. I'd told my mom previously that if the police ever showed up to her house, I would surrender peacefully. But now, all I could think of was how close I was to leaving Michigan. I broke out running for the side door. One of the officers that was standing on the front porch jumped over the rail and gave chase while the other one ran back to the car. I sprinted up the alley like my life depended on it. I had a huge lead on him, so I found a backyard to hide in. After about fifteen minutes, I tried to come out of hiding but by then, cops were everywhere.

I ran down the alley where I spotted two teenagers walking by. I guess the girl knew I was running from the cops, because she signaled for me to turn around and go back because they were coming my way. I ran and hid again. I came out to look about ten minutes later, and there were even more cops flying through my neighborhood searching for me. As I moved further down the alley, I was running out of places to hide.

I was trying to reach the backyard of a female friend. She was Boogie's ex-girlfriend, and I knew if I could just make it to her back door she'd let me in. I knew Lisa was probably circling the block looking for me by now, but I had no phone to call her. As I hid in a backyard, I started making too much noise and the homeowner heard me. They came out and spotted me hiding under their van. I knew they were going to tell on me. For all they knew, I could've been a serial rapist on the loose.

I took off down the alley and spotted more cops circling the block. I hid under a fruit crate and a bunch of tumble weed. I was determined to find my way out of this. As soon as I was hidden away, the police showed up in the backyard that I was just in hiding under the van. I could hear the homeowners were telling on me like I knew they would. I could hear every word they said. The police started to search the alley. My chances of making it out were looking scanty. It was hard to hide under a fruit crate. As the cop that chased me from the house started looking right in the area I was in, he was puzzled.

"He couldn't have gone too fucking far," he fumed.

The rest of the cops searched the backyard and found nothing. But the closer he walked to the tumble weed, I realized the heel of my shoe was sticking out. Seconds later, so did he as he snatched up the crate then me.

"Get yo' bitch ass up! You gon' make me chase you muthafucka!" he shouted.

He was still breathing hard and super pissed off. He threw the cuffs on me and started to ask me every stupid question he could think of.

"Why the fuck you run? You got something on you?"

If he thought he was angry, he must hadn't looked in my eyes. I was so mad I probably had smoke coming off me. I remember thinking if I'd had an AK, I'd aim it and kill every cop in sight. Thirty minutes later, I would've been in the wind. As they led me out to the street, there were about eight police cars parked on the connecting corner. They were all hi-fiving and cracking jokes, and all I kept thinking about was if I had a gun, I'd kill 'em all. I was mad they'd caught me when I was so close to getting away. I couldn't believe I was headed right back to jail.

There was so much that had gone wrong in such a short period of time that I could've never imagined before being released. Had I known back then how thoughts become things, I'm one hundred percent sure I could've turned that situation around for a more positive outcome. But because I knew nothing about the way the mind works, just how powerful the emotion of fear is, as soon as something went wrong, I panicked. That panic led to some of the worst decisions I'd ever made. Had I made a choice to just look for and expect the

FIGHT OF MY LIFE

best possible outcome, I'm sure things would've gone much different.

Would I have gone right back to prison only after two weeks of being home? Possibly, but now I realize that it would've probably been a two-to-five-month stay at the most, and I would've been back out in the streets. Instead, I was in for a ride much rougher than my first experience with prison.

THE REVOLVING DOOR

I WAS ONLY OUT OF PRISON about eight months total. Now I was right back in this same hellhole, trying to make sense of it all. I had to tell myself the only reason I was released in the first place was because my mother needed me at the time. Deep down inside, I felt my initial punishment didn't really fit the crime, so I tried to suck it up and do my time, but this would be a totally different journey.

The first three years of prison were easy. I'd learned a lot about myself and things outside of myself. I'd stood up to niggas doing life with nothing to lose and in my eyes, I solidified myself as a real gangsta. I finished school and got in the best shape of my young life. Now at twenty-five, I was about to travel down the same road all over again, and I couldn't see getting anything out of a second prison term but misery. For the most part, I was right.

I only had six months on my original sentence but because of my escape, I had to do an additional two years. That would've been easier if I'd known I was going to do another two and a half years going in, but I had to see the parole board four times before I would be released. Each time I had my hopes up high and each time I was denied, it took a small piece of my mental stability and wholeness. My stress level was so high after the second denial I had high blood pressure for a month or two. Still, there was nothing I could do about it but do the time for the crime.

I was spending my best years locked away from everything I loved. But even at my lowest point, I wasn't

FIGHT OF MY LIFE

thinking of leaving the game. See prison doesn't rehabilitate anyone no matter how hard the time is. The only thing that changes a person is their will to change. You have to want a different life for yourself. To me, I was still paying the dues of living life as a gangsta. I knew it wasn't always glamorous going in.

So I locked in on a schedule again and stayed as busy as possible. I took a computer class that I had no idea would be extremely valuable to me years later. I started to study Spanish and learned about real estate. I did whatever I could to make those two and half years go by and feel like I didn't just waste those years of my life. Some of those things helped build my confidence again, especially learning to speak Spanish. I realized once again I could still do whatever I set my mind to. Now I just had to learn how to apply it all to life outside of those gates. After two and half long, miserable years, I got parole and I was finally set free, but my mind was still on the game and getting all the money I missed out on. Now I felt like the game owed me.

FINALLY FREE

ONCE I WAS RELEASED FROM prison, I had a rejuvenated spirit. I'd become older and much wiser now. At twenty-seven, I figured if I was able to apply all the street knowledge along with the book smarts I'd learned in jail, I'd be rich in a few years. When I came home, I had a lot of support from my family and friends, which made the transition smoother. It felt good that I didn't have to rush off into anything because I felt like I needed the money. Every year I spent in prison, I felt like there was a knife being stuck further in my back, mainly because I knew I was so much more valuable to everyone I loved on the streets.

Now that I was out, I felt like that knife had finally been removed. I moved in with my sister, who was probably the most supportive all the years of my incarceration. For the first month, I just hung out with my family and friends, trying to readjust to all the changes the new millennium had brought with it.

My sister had a bunch of new friends she'd met while attending community college for her nursing degree. All of her friends were fine as hell, and I was trying to get to know them better. I had a chance to take advantage of my jail glow this time. It sounds crazy, but women really are drawn to guys when they come home from jail. Just ask anyone that's ever been. Most of my homies were doing good for themselves at this time, so it was nothing to get caught up on my gear. I hit the mall a few times, and I was good to go.

FIGHT OF MY LIFE

On the outside looking in, all the women I ran across were trying to figure me out. All they really knew was I was young, I'd just come home, and I stayed fresh jumping out of Benzes, Escalades, and Navigator trucks. I wasn't doing anything, but I always had money. The biggest change that really strengthened my support system was that my homey Kev that I was at camp with was home now and had come up big time. He didn't want me to rush into anything, but he assured me when the time was right, I was on. I knew the stress that came with the streets, so I really took the time to enjoy my freedom. I went to movies, plays, jazz concerts, and all the things I felt like a guy my age should be doing. I really enjoyed the first couple of months of freedom but after that, it was time to get to work. I called Kev and told him I was ready to get busy. I had to start supporting myself. I needed a car and crib.

He started me off with a couple of pounds, which I was grateful for. I hadn't been on the streets in years, so I wasn't expecting him to open up the floodgates to give me shit I couldn't move. I hooked up with a chick named Kyra that used to hustle for me back in the days. Her house would be the weed house. I broke a pound down and sold bags, and the rest I moved in weight. I went to the secretary of state and got my license so people wouldn't have a problem handing over their keys to me.

I was doing good on my end, but what I didn't know was the chick Kyra had developed a strong weed habit while I was gone away. She was smoking more than she was selling and kept making up excuses about where the money went. It was always something. She ran the woe is me game in the ground, so I just cut her off and kept moving weight. I didn't make as much moving weight but it was low key. The problem was, I had so much I wanted to do, I wasn't trying to be patient. I'd spent five and half years being patient, and I needed money coming faster than it was coming. After a few flips, I sold off all the weed and bought some crack. I appreciated what Kev was trying to do, but that weed just wasn't the right move for me at the time.

Once I got some coke, things started to make little more sense, but I had a long way to go. I was starting all the way over with trying to establish clientele, and the whole hood was hustling and fighting for what nowadays wasn't the same kind of money. I was really an unwelcomed addition for a lot of hustlers, but oh well. It was time for them to make room.

When I was locked up, I used to always think about this girl from my hood. Her name was Kisha and even though I knew she came from a pretty rough background, I figured with my background, who was I to judge? We had a lot of the basic ghetto shit in common, and she'd really grown up to be a beautiful young lady. She reminded me of the Kisha from the movie *Belly*. I told myself I would have her when I came home. It took me a minute to find out where she was staying but as soon as I did, I made my move. She was living with her sister at their dad's house, whom I knew from the hood. When I saw her for the first time in years, she was looking as good as I thought she would. She had smooth, chocolate skin and a beautiful grade of long, dark hair. I'd told her I'd been searching the city for her, and she just smiled at me with the most beautiful big eyes. I had to have her. I asked her out and we started dating.

With both of us being from the hood, everyone had an opinion about Kisha and I dating. I'd known her family since they were all kids. Her mom used to help me hustle from time to time. Her mom was a straight-up gangsta and she was one of the females in the hood that all the others knew not to fuck with. The word on the streets was Kisha was crazy just like her mother. But I already knew her story and I felt like I could handle her. I was used to dating gangsta chicks that sold dope and shot dice, so she couldn't be any worse.

We hit it off pretty good, and it didn't take long for me to realize that we had more in common than I thought. The

FIGHT OF MY LIFE

streets were right. Kisha had her mom's ways and she definitely had the heart to hustle. This was good news for me, and I immediately started to think of how I could capitalize on her ambition. Before I could come up with a proposition, she gave me one of her own.

"You should give me some of your stuff to sell, 'cause ain't nothing but fiends around here," she said one day while we were sitting outside in the truck I drove at the time.

I had nothing to lose, so I gave her a chance. It turned out to be the first really smart move I'd made since I'd been home. There wasn't as much money in my hood as it used to be, but her hood was banging with clientele. I didn't even have to pay her a lot because she made a killing on crediting a lot of her dope out until the first of the month. Since I was now working in two different hoods, one of us always had a good day.

Some days, she would move more work than I did. The hustle chemistry we had was pulling me closer to her. I was falling for this one and I was falling hard. I always wanted a chick I could get money with. Someone that could understand my lifestyle and roll with it. After a few months of dating and hustling together, we were official. We started discussing our living arrangements. She was tired of living with her dad and I was tired of living with my sister. At that point, it only made sense for us to get a place and move in together. We never actually said we were in a relationship, it just happened.

Once we were officially a couple, I told her she couldn't hustle anymore. I needed her to play a different role that wouldn't jeopardize her freedom. It was easy for her to agree with me. She had a two-year-old son and was ready to stop taking those kinds of chances anyway. About a month later, we found a house and moved in together. Up to that point, I'd never actually lived with a woman before. I would always have a set of keys to someone's house, but I spent most of my nights sleeping in crack spots and expensive hotels. It was always apex luxury or bottom barrel for me. I knew now that I'd moved in with someone, I'd taken on the responsibility of paying the bills.

I felt really good about this situation because we'd both started with nothing and we were building a future together. I liked the idea of coming home to home-cooked meals every night and never sleeping alone. Everything was going smoothly. I had a cool parole officer that never harassed me about anything. As long as I reported, dropped clean urine, and paid my restitution, she left me alone.

Now that my girl wasn't hustling anymore, I had to hustle extra hard to pick up the slack. I missed that extra income, but I couldn't allow her to take those chances anymore. I had to stay out later and later to make sure all the bills were paid. She did hair and made money on side hustles, but I was the bread winner, so I had to make it happen regardless. I never asked her to work back then because I wanted her to be the girl that kept me organized. I still needed her to chop rocks, pick up money, wash the clothes, cook, and keep the house clean. Call me old fashioned, but she sure didn't mind one bit.

As hard as I was hustling, I still needed more money. It just wasn't a lot of money in the hood slanging crack anymore. I mean, all the bills were getting paid, but I didn't see any real progress. By now, my brother had come home and he was helping Hammer sell weed on the same block he'd been on forever. Hammer finally caught a case and his lawyer advised him to stay away from the block until the case was settled. Hammer left the block and opened up a record store.

As a gesture of loyalty for all the years they'd been down together, Hammer gave my brother Black and his cousin the weed house and put them on with a package. The only catch was Hammer still sold weight, so Black would have to buy directly from him if he was going to hustle on his block. Around this time, the weed house had slowed down. It had gone from three pounds a day to less than a pound, but it was still very profitable. Hammer's cousin that he put on didn't last

FIGHT OF MY LIFE

long. He fell off the same month. Black wasn't too far behind him. He couldn't maintain enough money and product to keep the house going. He'd run out of weed all the time and miss more money than he made.

I saw there was a problem with supply and demand. I knew my man Kev would still hit me with whatever I needed for a cheaper price. Now here's where I have to explain the ethical part of my next decision. Although Hammer had looked out for me and Black on several occasions, he'd also screwed us over just as many times, but I won't go into the details. Let's just say that Hammer always was and always will be the kind of guy that disappeared for weeks, sometimes months, if he wasn't ready to pay you what he owed. We had all looked out for each other at one time or another because that's what friends do but in the game, sometimes it was every man for himself.

Hammer wasn't making money at the record store or on the block. He couldn't afford to stay on, so he couldn't afford to supply Black in a timely manner, even when Black did have the money. The main reason my brother wasn't making any money was because he'd have to sit and wait for days until Hammer could produce some more weed. Black would hand over all his money to Hammer and then just sit, wait, and watch day after day as all the loyal customers continued to show up and leave disappointed. It was turning the block into a ghost town. I stayed out of it at first, but after Black's constant complaining, it only made sense to make a move.

My nigga Kev had an unlimited supply of weed, and I needed to make more money than I was making. I called Kev and he came through and put me on again. Of course, this would mean that Black and I were now partners in the weed game. Hammer was steaming mad when he found out. I guess he had every right to be, but when you looked at it from our perspective, my brother would've gone broke had he continued down the path Hammer laid out for him. It was business not personal, and we knew if the shoe was on the other foot, Hammer wouldn't have hesitate to make the same move.

Business began to pick up after that because the house was being supplied properly but a couple weeks later, Black got arrested for a counterfeit bill in Warren, MI. He didn't know the money he passed was fake, I'm sure someone slid it to him in the dark, but police didn't care. He was a black man in the suburbs with fake money. Around this same time, I met a mixed kid name Zo that looked like just like Bizzy Bone. Zo had bounced around from state to state and somehow landed in Detroit. He really didn't have a place to stay when we met, so he spent a lot of time around the weed house with one of Hammer's cousins.

Black had a warrant for parole violation, so he couldn't get out with that parole hold on him. With Hammer and Black gone, that left me to hold down the block. I ran it the same way Hammer ran it. Twenty-four-seven selling nothing but dime bags. Things picked up faster and before long, I was selling whatever customers wanted. The more pounds I bought, the more I got fronted. I hired Zo and bought Sal in to help out. Sal hired Hammer's cousin to work for him. Sal was having money problems at the time, and it felt good that I could help him with his situation. It also felt good to see that my hustle hand was still intact. I hadn't built this block, but I definitely kept it from being ran into the ground.

After being home for about seven months, I got myself a car and new wardrobe. I knew I had to look out for my girl too, because Christmas was right around the corner and she'd been helping with everything I was doing. All of her friends and family got their weed from me and she would make small runs to them from time to time. When Christmas came, I bought her a whole new wardrobe as well and looked out for her son, who was quickly becoming my stepson by his father not being around. I bought all my nieces and nephews' gifts and my mom a television. On New Year's Eve, I stayed home

FIGHT OF MY LIFE

with my girl and we popped bottles of champagne. If felt good to be back in action.

I'd been home for less than a year when I started to get a wandering eye and more temptation from the girls in my hood. I started creeping with this bad little chick from around my way. Her sex was so good I started seeing her on a regular. She even gave me my first threesome. Life was definitely good, and I was finally feeling like myself again. Nobody could tell me I wasn't the hustler I thought I was, because this run I was getting had confirmed it. I'd taken a dying block and revived it full swing. But the game was always a rollercoaster ride, and what goes up must come down. Just like that, as soon as I started to get comfortable, bad things started to happen.

First, somebody peeped my stash in the vacant house across the street and stole a sizable amount of weed. Then, the narcs caught me slipping a couple weeks later and robbed my weed house for all the money and weed. Then, the house got raided and Zo caught a pistol case. Once the police found a gun in the house, they raided the house for a week straight. We had no choice but to shut down, and I went from making thousands a day to making no money at all. I wasn't selling crack anymore because I didn't have to. The weed house was all the income I had.

When Zo got out of jail, he left the city, which meant I had to hustle my own weed. The only place I could really make some money was that hot ass block I'd been on from the start. It was dead of winter, but I had bills to pay, so I stood out on the block the same way I did when I was selling crack. By now, most of the houses in my hood were burned down, so it wasn't easy to just up and relocate a spot. I had no choice but to tough it out in the cold. But the real nail in the coffin was when Hammer popped back up on the block. He was broke and desperate for money himself.

The block was hot and slow. There wasn't enough money for me, nevertheless enough to split between the two of us, but

KING BENJAMIN

what could I do? It was literally his block that he'd built from the ground up over years and years. If he wanted to come hustle, he had that right. So now it was both of us outside every day catching whatever we could before police came snooping. Shortly after that, Black came home from his small stint in county jail. He felt like I owed him money because he left me with his weed. I gave him exactly what he left me and nothing more. The come up I'd made had been wiped away. I'd taking nothing but losses for the past month. There was no way he was about to make a profit for sitting in jail, but he didn't see it that way.

He was really upset that I'd caught a run after he was incarcerated, but the truth was, I'd spent that money already and I couldn't get it back. I was getting frustrated with the block and everybody on it. A few days later, a young guy from my neighborhood ran into my car. He said he would pay for the damages or steal me a bumper to replace mine. I agreed to his terms. A week goes by and I don't hear anything from him. Every time I see him, I ask him about the money or the car he was supposed to steal, and he'd spin me.

I was feeling really disrespected being that I was OG in my hood now and he was a young pup. One day, I saw him at the stop light in a black Mustang. The same one he was in the day he hit me. I told Black who was in the passenger seat and that I was about to shoot him today if he didn't have my money. I pulled up on him and rolled my window down, but he was on Black's side.

"What's up, nigga? You gon' give me my money or what?" I said.

He waved me off with his hand, saying fuck me. I reached for my gun.

"Give to me," Black said.

He was closer, so I gave it to him as the youngin' tried to drive off. Black aimed the gun and opened fire, but the

FIGHT OF MY LIFE

youngin' escaped with just a few broken windows out of his Mustang. I didn't really consider this a beef, I just wanted my money. I was already stressing and him hitting my car was just another headache adding to my problems. The next morning, I got a call from a big money customer. He said he was on the block and that he would wait on me. I went to the block and made the sale.

I didn't realize I didn't have my gun on me until after I'd made it to the hood. I was about to go back home and get it, but the first corner I turned, I ran right into the youngin' we'd shot at the night before. Of course, he had his gun now. He started shooting. I don't know what he shot at, because he didn't hit anything remotely close to me or my car. It was almost funny after I got home.

I'd put myself in that situation by going out unprepared. It could've turned out a lot worse, but I vowed to never let it happen again. I didn't know it then, but everything that was happening was just guiding me into a new direction and much better opportunity. It was time for a new start.

HUSTLE REAL HARD

AFTER THE INCIDENT WITH THE young gun, I decided to lay low from the hood until my name cooled down. Everyone in the hood knew what was going on by now. I had every intention of killing him, but I was still on parole and couldn't afford to be hot headed and stupid. I had to put some time between the incidents before he came up dead. I sold weed around the area I lived in, and to the small clientele I'd built, but it wasn't enough money to make a come up. I noticed that the neighborhood was flooded with dope fiends and crack addicts more than anything. I was back in the area I was born in. The Black Bottom.

When I realized what a gold mine it was, I knew I was going to put something down eventually. The more I thought about, I couldn't wait. The time was now. I had nothing going on but a slow weed grind. I started looking for a crack house in the area. After a lot of plotting and strategizing, I realized I wasn't going to come up on a house so easily. All the people I knew in the area at the time had no desire or ability to do any hustling. I didn't know any of the smokers, but that was the easy part. I decided I had to go old school with it.

I copped some work and went and copped a pager that same day. The small amount of crack I could afford was just enough to cut some big rocks and make a name for myself quickly. I wasn't concerned about the profit at that point, just getting my name ringing in the area. I drove around the hood rolling up on every assumed smoker I could find, telling them

FIGHT OF MY LIFE

who I was and how they could reach me. I passed out samples, knowing that was the only real way to get their attention.

I gave out a lot of drugs, but by the end of the day, my networking paid off. Most of the people I gave the beeper number to had probably lost the number within an hour of me giving it to them. Smokers can't be expected to be responsible with that kind of thing. I met a white girl that looked too young to be out on the strip, but she'd been out there all day every day for the past week. When I approached her, she immediately pulled on the car door and hopped in the backseat. She had no fear of me being a cop or out to rob her. All she wanted to know was what I had for sale as she produced a wad of cash. I sold her a few rocks and that was the beginning of a long lasting and profitable relationship.

"What's your name?" I asked.

"My name's Roxanne," she replied.

"My name Buggs," I revealed.

I didn't know it then, but I'd just made a connection with the biggest money making hoe on the strip and the person that sparked the momentum of my comeback in the dope game. Roxanne was really attractive and only about twenty-one when I met her. I happened to live right down the street from where she stood on the hoe stroll all day in front of the liquor store. She bought drugs all day every day. I could've probably got by on the money Roxanne spent alone because she would buy and sell some to her friends and come right back.

My dope was good, and the rocks were so big, she'd cut them in half and sell them to all the smokers who didn't know me yet. She was the only one that held on to the beeper number, so everybody that wanted my dope had to go through her. It wasn't long before everyone was saying I had the best shit in the neighborhood. Once they realized that Roxanne was the only one that had access to me, they all felt left out and turned green with envy.

KING BENJAMIN

Soon, they all had memorized my face and I couldn't walk to the liquor store without three or four smokers crowded around me begging for the beeper number. I gave it out all over again but this time, they guarded it with their lives. They carried the number around everywhere, just waiting to get enough money to page me. After hitting a lick, they'd walk to the phone both across from the liquor store and page me with the code. After a couple weeks, they just got downright disrespectful and wrote the number inside the payphone.

There was a spot next to the liquor store we called the Crack Park. When I saw my pager number on the phone booth, I went to the Crack Park and threatened everyone inside. Having my pager number on the inside of a phone booth was like an open invitation for somebody to come rob me. This hood was flooded with wolves.

"Call him and leave this code and he's gonna show up with a bag full of crack!" they might as well had said.

Not only was this plan of mine risky as hell, it was like I'd traveled back into the early nineties or something. The time had been passed for working off of pagers, but it was working out way better than I could've imagined. I hustled all day and night, running to the corner to meet people. There was never any sleep during this process because the smokers never slept, and I couldn't afford to miss out on any money. Maybe once a week I would just pass out and miss the money but other than that, I was on it.

After a couple of months of straight grinding, things got out of control. Customers began knocking on my door and whistling outside of my house in the middle of the night. I couldn't even get in the car with my girl and her son without someone trying to flag me down or run behind my car. I knew something had to give. I was making good money again, but I was putting my house in jeopardy of being raided.

FIGHT OF MY LIFE

Soon, my landlord came to visit and basically accused me of selling drugs out of the house. I assured him that wasn't the case and whoever told him that probably had an ulterior motive. He told me one of the people he got his information from was the sergeant of the police precinct in that area. At that point, I decided to go the honest route.

"Look, man, I do what I do around the neighborhood, but what I do around here has nothing to do with this house. This where I lay my head."

He told me whatever I was doing to make the sergeant think otherwise, I needed to clean it up fast. His concern was the same as mine. The house getting raided and torn up by police looking for drugs. I definitely agreed with his position, so I came up with a way to keep getting money and get the police off of my trail. By now, Black was living with me and he had nothing but time on his hands. I decided we should work as a tag team. The Crack Park was wide open and just as risky, but it was big money sitting right in our faces.

All the people that called me from the phone booth went right to the Crack Park to sit and get high. My brother would set up shop right in the park from morning until nightfall. That way, nobody was paging me while the sergeant was working his shift. When it got dark, I would take over from there and go back to working from the pager.

That move was more successful than the beeper was. All the people that didn't have the patience to go page a dealer and then wait on him had access to good dope right there on deck. It seemed like the word just kept spreading and people were coming from ten and twelve blocks away to get the dope they'd been hearing about in the Crack Park. I don't want to make it sound like I was making an astronomical amount of money. I was making about fifteen hundred dollars a day at that point, but when you take in the fact that the average smoker was only spending ten dollars at a time, it was an extreme amount of traffic right out in the open.

KING BENJAMIN

Plus, I had to factor in that technically, I wasn't even from around here. I wasn't supposed to be able to come in this hood and put it down like this, because someone had to be feeling their pockets getting a lighter. I wasn't the first or the last to put it down in the Crack Park, and once business really picked up, everyone warned me that the police would probably be raiding the park soon like they did every summer.

There wasn't much we could do about the inevitable raid but be careful and try to not get caught with anything. One thing for sure, I'm positive that my run at the Crack Park was the longest of anyone that ever had the balls to do it. On a rainy day, about two days before my birthday, two police vans raided the park and my brother was there. He got caught with a small amount of drugs. He told me later that they raided the park as soon as he got there, not giving him time to stash the drugs. This let me know that the police had to still be watching me. At that point, I stopped holding anything at my house, realizing I was still on parole and couldn't risk it. My brother was also on parole, so he went back to prison for violating with a new charge.

I felt bad for him because he'd started making good money with me and for the first time in a long time, we were getting along. I told my girl that we really needed to start looking for a house so we could move as soon as possible. After a few days, I actually went back to the Crack Park to get off the rest of my bag. I couldn't just sit by and watch all the smokers sitting up there with a pocket full of money and no drugs. I was nervous as hell though. Every car that drove by with a white guy in it looked like an undercover to me.

I couldn't do that beeper thing in the daytime, so I eventually started just working the night shift. I carried my pistol every time I went to the phone booth, and I made sure everyone knew they had to be spending some real money if they paged me. In the morning, I'd take all the dope and guns out of the house.

FIGHT OF MY LIFE

It was all becoming a painstaking process, but I knew I couldn't go anywhere and punch a clock to get the money I was making. One day, I went to the liquor store and a smoker asked me to come to his house, saying he wanted to show me something. I went to his so-called house, which was really a garage with electricity. He had the garage set up with furniture, carpet, and cable TV. He said if I wanted, I could set up shop right there. I knew I needed to get away from that corner and the Crack Park fast. I was willing to try my luck with just about anything to keep this flow going. I was missing too much money only working at night.

I set up shop the very next day and once again, the smokers flooded the spot from everywhere. Just like the park was better than the pager, the garage was even better than both of them. I started pumping twenty-five hundred dollars of day in crack out of this tiny garage right on the corner of Kirby and Chene. I immediately hired help to sit there and sling for me. I moved out of the house I had on Chene and into a house off Seven Mile. I bought a new car and started cruising Van Dyke looking for the young dude that shot at me.

Every time I came through, I'd be in a different car so people couldn't tell him what I was driving. Enough time had passed now, and I had every intent on killing him for shooting at me. He turned out to be harder to find than I'd expected. It was nice outside and everyone was out and about, but this dude was nowhere to be found. After a few weeks, I grew tired of looking but I made sure I was strapped every time I went through the hood.

As good as things were going at the garage, deep down, I knew that wouldn't last either. It was too much traffic coming to this little ass garage right off Chene. Just way too obvious, but it was all I had to work with. We tried running the traffic through the back alley, but that only bought us a little more time. One night, I took my guy Jimmy that was helping me out for his birthday.

KING BENJAMIN

Everything about this night was beautiful. We went to the mall and got fresh from head to toe. We both had a pocket full of money, feeling like all the hard work was paying off. I also met a beautiful woman that night, and I remember thinking life was about to get really good. Then, the next night, Jimmy got caught in the garage when the narcs raided. Then, something really strange happened. When he went in front of the judge, there was no record of the dope or the gun he was supposedly charged with because of a mix up with him having two last names. He was let out without any record of the two felonies. Since he got away Scott free, Jimmy went right back to slinging in the garage while I searched for somewhere to relocate.

We were way too hot but still greedy for the money. Even when the narcs weren't rolling, the raid van was creeping by. Sometimes we'd come in the hood and ride by the garage and the narcs would already be up in the spot harassing the smoker who lived there. We laid low for a minute, but when I couldn't come up with a new spot, the money was calling me back. Twenty-five hundred a day was hard to walk away from. I was moving a half a brick a week. Jimmy was there ninety percent of the time, so he endured most of the risk.

But one night, Jimmy had the day off and as I drove by the garage, all I could see was smokers roaming like zombies looking for crack. I couldn't let it all pass, and I had no one else to work the spot. I went and grabbed a sack and came back to get it off myself. The traffic was coming so fast, I was thinking about the narcs the entire time. The realization that the police could come kicking on the door any minute was a constant nagging in my brain. A smoker came to cop on a motorcycle. I was conversing with him about the bike, asking him to let me ride it. After I sold him the rocks, we continued to talk about the bike as he walked toward the door.

Instead of my doorman looking outside to make sure the coast was clear before he opened it, he just opened the door and the narcs walked right in on me with the sack still in my

FIGHT OF MY LIFE

hand. I was back smoking weed now and the weed I'd smoked earlier slowed my reaction time. If not for that, I would've made a run for it, but instead, I froze up. They pointed guns, telling me to drop the bag and I did. They threw the cuffs on me fast and all I could think about was I still had five months of parole left to do. I had only been home 19 months. I had no realistic angle to fight the case, being caught red handed, and not a chance in hell at receiving probation. Even if I could get probation, my P.O. would still violate me. I was going back to prison.

Down at the precinct, I sat in a cell disgusted with myself. How could I be so stupid to go back in there after they'd raided the spot more than once? I didn't even need the money, and now I was on my way back to prison for being stupid. Some people reading this might think Jimmy set me up, but trust me, if Jimmy wanted to set me up, I would've never seen the streets again.

As I continued to curse myself, I remembered one thing that my brother had told me. When I talked to him in the county, he'd told me that his parole officer, which was also my parole officer, never knew about his arrest. She'd only found out after he'd given me the okay to tell her, assuming she already knew. He had so much child support he owed it would've been impossible to make bond anyway. But there was nothing stopping me from making bond if I didn't have a parole hold.

I definitely wasn't telling anybody I was on parole. If they didn't know, they'd have to do some police work and find out for themselves. If my plan worked, I could be back on the streets in a couple days. If it didn't work, I was headed to do some time that was going to be extremely taxing on me physically and mentally. I'd gotten high blood pressure the last time I was in this situation.

This time, I didn't bother God, begging him to get me out of trouble again or even pray about it. I just decided if it was

KING BENJAMIN

my time to go back to jail, I would go and if not, I wouldn't. Somehow, it worked. I went in front of a judge and was freed on a personal bond for the second time in my life. The police had taken all of my money, so I walked all the way from the precinct back to the block my car was parked on. I hopped in and drove off, headed home. I felt like I was having the best luck and worst luck at the same time. I was free when I was supposed be on a parole hold, but I was also about to go on the run again.

SOME KIND OF LOVE

SEVERAL MONTHS BEFORE MY ARREST, my girl announced she was pregnant, which was one of the reasons I was hustling so hard. For me, this was absolutely the best news I'd gotten my whole life. I knew a child would bring me a joy I'd never known. By this time, I'd become really attached to her son, and the fact that his biology father wasn't around and now he had a sibling on the way just confirmed for me that I would be the man to raise him.

One day, I sat him down and we had a long talk. Afterwards, I told him he could call me Dad from that point on. I'd been playing the role all along, but now I wanted him to know that I'd accepted that role in his life. He was a bad ass little boy at a terrible two and half, but he was my son, and he'd brought me a lot of joy even before my child came. Now, all of sudden, one night had changed everything. There was no way I was leaving my girl with two kids to raise on her own. We had to pack up and move again so that once I stopped reporting, my parole officer wouldn't have an address to find and arrest me.

I still went to report a couple times while we looking for a house. Each time I was super nervous, but I didn't want a warrant out before I could move. She never mentioned the drug case but soon, my first court date came for it and I'd be a no show for court and for my parole officer. Here I was, for the third time in my life, on the run from the law. This time it

KING BENJAMIN

didn't bother me as much because I had some money and a solid plan to keep me out of jail for a long time.

Hustling became harder without a spot, but the good thing was I had made a strong name for myself. I could move around the streets and make a killing hand to hand. If I came to the neighborhood with drugs, I never left with anything but a pocket full of cash. I wasn't afraid to post up anywhere because now I had nothing to lose. Soon, the weather started to change and it was getting too cold to stand outside selling dope.

One day, while I was on the streets hustling, a grimy, old school fiend named Big Smoke approached me about buying some dope. He was driving a hooptie and I told him I had it with me. I knew what type of dude Big Smoke was, but never in a million years did I think he'd try me. I figured at his age, he was retired from the grimy shit.

As he pulled over, I never paid attention to the two guys in the backseat because I was too busy watching for the cops. The next thing I knew, the first guy was getting out and upping a AK-47. I never considered running because I knew what they wanted. It wasn't worth the risk. The drugs and the money I had on me was less than a thousand dollars. Big Smoke stayed in the car while a third guy walked towards me without a weapon.

"Give me all that shit, cuz," he ordered.

I looked at the guy posted up next to the car with an AK, making sure I remembered his face. I gave up all the money and drugs I had on me, and they went on their merry way. So now, I had two guys on my hit list to shoot on sight. The youngster and Big Smoke. The guys that robbed me weren't from that hood. There was no telling when I'd see them again, but knew I'd see Big Smoke again sooner or later. I knew how he got down, so I cursed myself for not having my gun, but I couldn't afford a pistol case on top of everything else. I hadn't

FIGHT OF MY LIFE

put down any plays in the Black Bottom to let niggas know not to test me, so I knew eventually someone would. Okay, cool.

After that, I combed the hood until I found my first real crack house. I couldn't hustle on the strip with a gun on me. I'd face a minimum of five years if I got caught on top of the drug charge and parole violation. So that robbery closed that chapter of hustling on the strip, which turned out to be a good thing because it forced me to move smarter. As soon as I found a house, of course, the guns came back out. I found a really good way to securely hide them from police, and it was on.

I worked the spot with Jimmy the first few weeks. I knew people needed to see my face on the scene, so they knew it was really my spot. The very first week, I had to let my Tech-9 off at a nigga that was pissed because I'd smacked his shady ass girlfriend for giving me fake money. Trust me, she had it coming and so did he. After another incident with Jimmy, word spread that we had an arsenal and I was able to hustle in peace.

I knew it was time I started letting people know exactly who I was and how I ran my operations. Every once in a while, I'd still have to beat a nigga's ass or pistol whip somebody for trying to play us. But before long, nobody came to the spot with bold business for fear of the repercussions. So, things were going good and now I could kick back while Jimmy worked the spot, and we both ate pretty good. This spot did over three thousand dollars a day for quite a long time, and I never saw the police even ride up the block. It was quiet and cool, just like I liked it. Most days I'd just come by to pick up the money and go back home, being that my girl was in her third trimester and needed me there at the house more. Since I'd been on the run, I went to great lengths to make sure I was around to see my daughter come into the world.

The day her mom went into labor, I remember driving her to the hospital with sweaty hands, I was so excited. By now I had a fake ID and drove everywhere without the fear of being pulled over. I called everyone I could think of to tell them the

KING BENJAMIN

great news. My girl's mother was there taking pictures of her before she went into labor. The one thing I will never forget was the moment my daughter came into the world.

The process of birthing a child is one of the most mind-blowing things I've ever seen. I just couldn't believe what I was watching. It was honestly overwhelming, and it was something that I relished the first time, but never wanted to see it again. No words could describe the way I felt the first time holding my daughter in my arms. My sense of purpose immediately grew stronger than ever before. All I could think about was my beautiful daughter and my handsome son. Nothing else seemed to matter but my family.

That was when I realized I could really get used to the family life. I enjoyed coming home to them every night. I enjoyed coming home seeing my son run up in his pajamas right before we started to play fight. I enjoyed holding my daughter every night, seeing her smile when I would hold her. I knew there was no amount of money that would give me that feeling, but I also knew I didn't want my kids growing up struggling. Although having kids turned me into a family man of sorts, for a short period in time, it was also my justification to turn best friends with Satan.

While Jimmy ran the spot, I sat at home changing diapers, being the best dad I could be. At night, I would watch them sleep, thinking about their future. I knew I didn't want them raised in an environment that I had accepted for myself. I thought about what it would be like if they were part of a generation that was able to start a different cycle. I knew both my family and my girl's family were still traveling down a road that didn't seem to have a bright future, but I expected more from her and myself. I wanted to be the one to break the generational poverty. My family tree wasn't pretty. All my aunts and uncles on my mom's side had been to prison or suffered from mental illness.

FIGHT OF MY LIFE

Even my mom had a break down when I was younger. I remember us being shipped off to Mississippi one summer while she got herself together. I remember thinking my mom and my aunt looked so much alike at that age, I barely knew the difference. So, I basically had no real reason to believe that I would have a bright future, other than my burning desire to win. I just knew that my personal goal to be a much better man than my father never changed.

For me, that started with being the best man I could be for my children and at the time, that meant providing. I told myself I needed to secure their future at all cost. I wanted college funds put away as well as money put away in a trust fund. So eventually, when business started to slow down, I went into a panic. I had two kids to raise now. I couldn't afford to go back to just paying bills. I had too much on the line now. I did what I could to get the spot to pick back up, but nothing seemed to be working. Before long, I was thinking of a plan B that involved guns and ski masks.

DEALS WITH THE DEVIL

ONCE IT BECAME PAINFULLY OBVIOUS I was stuck at a standstill, I decided it was time to take action. By this time, armed robbery definitely wasn't new to me. I never again made the kind of sloppy and regrettable decisions I made at twenty-five, but if opportunity knocked and I needed the cash, I'd answer. I still didn't have the coping skills to deal with the threat of a struggle. I never forgot the day I went without eating. So once in a while, when the drug dealer wasn't doing so good, the stick-up kid in me would emerge.

Once I had kids to feed, it seemed like I took on robbery almost as a second job. I was tired of the rollercoaster ride the game was dishing out, so I did what I had to do to speed up the process of financial security. The first person I robbed was one of the barbers that used to cut my hair at the time. I'd done a few weed deals with him during our relationship, so he was comfortable with me.

One day, I called him up for a couple of pounds, knowing he wouldn't have any more than that. He didn't even have the two pounds, but he told me he could get it for me with a phone call. The whole purpose of me asking for the two was so I wouldn't have to involve anybody else that I didn't know. My barber wasn't really about that life. I wouldn't have to look over my shoulder after robbing him.

FIGHT OF MY LIFE

Now it was going in a direction that might turn out different. I decided to go through with it anyway. Since it was a small lick, I'd do it all alone and keep all the profits. I told myself if I had to rob them both, I would. After waiting about forty-five minutes, the barber called and I drove to his house. I didn't even take enough money with me to pretend like I was going to purchase the weed. I took my phone and my gun. I could only hope things didn't become too complicated and I end up risking my life over two pounds.

When I arrived, the guy we were waiting for wasn't there. He was in the area waiting for me to arrive first. Smart man, I thought. When he got there, he arrived in a brand-new Corvette. I thought to myself, there's no way my car is gonna outrun a Corvette. My barber got the weed from him and came over and jumped in my passenger seat. I opened one of the Ziplock bags and smelled the weed to make sure it was worth my money, of course. The weed was so strong I wished I'd put in an order for more. I pulled out my pistol.

"Get the fuck out," I said calmly.

His eyes grew big with shock. He was stunned, but he still tried to reason with me for a few seconds. I told him he was on the verge of being shot, and he quickly gathered all the motivation he needed to hurry up out of my shit. I knew at this point, the guy in the Corvette wasn't paying any attention to this ordinary transaction, because it was all in the routine day of a hustler. I started my car and took off as fast as I could. I remember driving so fast I fishtailed at the corner and had to get control of the wheel.

I could only guess the guy in the Corvette found out shortly after and decided it wasn't worth the chase for a couple pounds. For me, it was a cool come up. If I sold every ounce for $300 a pop, I'd have close to ten thousand, all free money. After that stick up, I decided I should raise the stakes if I was going to be out here risking my life. But the next lick, I didn't even need a gun for. I convinced another guy I never liked to

KING BENJAMIN

go in on a package with me, but I kept all the drugs for myself. When he came around asking for the money or some dope, I told him it all got caught up in a raid. He wasn't a friend of mine and he wasn't someone I trusted, so why he trusted me, I'll never know.

I never in my life turned on a friend, but during this time, I was truly moving like a wolf. I'd been preyed on before, and now I was on the hunt for prey. A few months passed and I still wasn't doing as good as I should've been. It was like one month I was winning and the next month I was taking losses. I was watching guys becoming successful seemingly overnight, but I was stuck at a standstill. Being a thousandaire was cool, but I wanted millions and I had to start somewhere.

My next lick was a lot more calculated, and I took every precautionary measure to make sure it went off without a hitch. The plug I was getting my coke from had started to really shit on me. He was the main reason the spot was slowing down. He was selling me powder that was always coming up short because it had been played with. Sometimes, he'd only have hard crack waiting to get all his money out of the streets to re-up. If I bought the hard, it was always wet, which meant I lost money, or it was played with and the smokers would complain about the taste.

I realized he was only out for himself and had no interest in seeing me prosper. If he wasn't with me, he was against me. I was moving about a brick and a half a month through my spot until his bullshit started slowing me down, but he didn't seem to care. One day I put in an order for a half a kilo. He only had fifteen ounces left but I told him bring it all. When he arrived with the dope, I pulled out on him, wasting no time. As usual, he tried to reason, but it was something about the barrel of a gun aimed at your head that makes you just cooperate. As I drove away, I realized I'd turned into the evilest version of myself I'd ever known.

FIGHT OF MY LIFE

I was acting like I had a death wish. I mean, this was a guy that could put a hit out on me or anything. But the devil had control of me, and I justified everything by telling myself I had a family to feed, and they wouldn't grow up poor like I did. I was determined to break the cycle. But the cycle I was on was worse, and it continued until my crack business picked up again and I didn't have to rob anymore. Even after I stopped, I still had to wear a bulletproof vest every day. I remember talking to Sal and him telling me to slow down before I got myself in a situation where I sped up my own death.

I'd told all my friends the truth about my hitting licks when I did it. I didn't want something jumping off in the streets with them because of something I did that they weren't aware of. But my spot was doing numbers again, and I even had a second house I'd opened up on the opposite end of the Chene and 94, closer to the freeway. I was finally getting money and I wasn't even splurging, because I knew at some point I had to go away. I had that part right. I always knew what was really important. I always had lawyer fees and money put to the side to bury me if I left the house one day and never came back.

At its peak, my first real spot on Chene was doing an eighth of a kilo every day and there wasn't a police or raid van in sight. Then I had the other house doing a slow roll, but it still added to the pot consistently. It felt so good to be a success, no matter how I was getting it. I was getting a small portion of what I thought the game owed me and I felt like a winner. That was all I wanted, to win. But, as usual, the game still came with its challenges.

During this time, almost all the dope boys were playing in the dope and selling bullshit. Almost seventy percent of the time I bought powder from a guy, the coke was stepped on or compressed, which meant it probably had been played with and put back together. If I bought it hard, eight times out of ten, it was wet. If I wasn't trying to slow my roll, I would've robbed them all, but I didn't need to rob at this point. I just needed good drugs at a decent price to keep the houses going.

KING BENJAMIN

When the weather was nice again, Big Smoke, the dude that robbed me on the strip, resurfaced in the hood. He was riding with a friend, sitting in the backseat of the car parked in front of the house. My dog spotted him first.

"Ain't that Big Smoke?" he asked me.

I turned to look and sure enough, there was Big Smoke sitting in the back seat with his mean mug on like he was a straight-up gangsta. He didn't see me, but I saw him. We pulled over immediately because I happened to be right in front of a close friend's house that I was sure had an AK in the closet. I knocked on the door and he opened it quickly.

"You still got that chopper?" I asked with urgency.

"Hell yeah," he replied.

I gave him the quick rundown and he did exactly what I knew he would. He led me to the closet and gave me the chopper. As I carried the assault rifle down the side of the house, I remembered there was a smoker in the hood that was driving around in a brand-new stolen car. He was a car thief so he always had a stolen car, but this was perfect timing. I went straight to his house and told him I'd pay him for the car because I wasn't bringing it back. He gave up the car with no questions asked.

I was with my homeboy Brick who just happened to only have one good eye—he was completely blind in the other. I'd never seen it effect his driving and I needed a driver, so I said fuck it. First, we went and changed our clothes. We put on all-black jeans and black hoodies. By the time we did all of that, of course, the car was gone from where I first spotted it.

We drove around looking for it and checking for police in the area at the same time. Once we saw the coast was clear, we came back to the block we'd spotted the car, and there it was sitting on the same block at a different location. Brick pulled down in the car slowly as I spotted my target all alone in the backseat. My guess was the other occupants had gone

FIGHT OF MY LIFE

inside. Lucky for them, I thought, as Brick pulled alongside, and I stuck the chopper out of the window.

Instead of stopping right where Big Smoke was at, Brick's blind ass drove past the car then stopped. That meant I had to stick my torso out of the window and aim backward, giving Big Smoke a chance to try and get low. I let off at least six thunderous rounds as Big Smoke tried to squeeze his huge frame on the floor of the backseat. The windows on the car shattered and collapsed inside the vehicle as I let off another few rounds. With each round, I could still see his body jerking from the enormous gun blast, but I couldn't tell if he was jerking from the sound of gunfire or injury. I readjusted my body and aimed again, letting off a few more rounds. I really wanted this nigga dead, but I was in a super awkward position shooting backwards.

After I was sure I'd gotten him, I slid back inside the car and Brick pulled off. I took the car to another hood, cleaned it, and dumped it after getting rid of the gun. An hour later, I was right back in the hood like nothing happened. I knew that no one had a clue who had launched this attack, and I was just waiting for someone in the neighborhood to walk up and tell me that Big Smoke was dead.

But the fact that I'm telling you this story should let you know that's not what happened at all. Somehow, by the mercy and grace of God, Big Smoke escaped the assault without a scratch. All those shots went everywhere but inside of him. The only thing I hurt was some guy's fancy car. It took weeks for me to find out he wasn't dead, but I just couldn't understand it. I knew I wasn't the best shot in the world, but this was ridiculous. Then I realized my own car had been shot up with a chopper and I also left without a scratch.

I surmised if it's not your time, it's not your time. It took me a long time to accept the fact that I'd missed the chance to kill Big Smoke, but I'd never stop trying. I was living life like I

KING BENJAMIN

was best friends with the devil, and anyone that wanted to cross me would pay the ultimate price sooner or later.

The incident did let me know that I was still very capable of murder at any given moment. So after that, I started offering my services as a hit man for hire. I was willing to do whatever it would take to come up and never come down again. I figured bad shot or not, if I get up close range, I won't miss, and I'd come up a lot quicker off hits than I would slinging coke. I would do anything as long as I could sleep at night after it was done. I definitely didn't have a problem sleeping after gunplay. Eventually, somebody took me up on my offer, but the guys who had a hit out on them ended up getting locked up before I could find them.

I never got a chance to live out the life of a hit man. After that, I went back to focusing on fast drug money. I just wanted to stack a few hundred grand and get out of the game before my own luck ran out. After doing so much dirt, I had to look at my karma as a real possibility. I wanted to stick around to raise my kids, but I knew it was a possibility that wasn't going to happen, so my main focus was to leave them a big chunk of money behind, mistakenly thinking it could replace a father's guidance. I still would look for big scores that would put me closer to my goals but mostly I focused on the hustle. Even though I was at my lowest as far as my soul was concerned, somehow God was watching over me the entire time.

DEVINE INTERVENTION

MY LIFE HAD BECOME THE exact opposite of what I'd planned for myself when I was locked up. I was supposed to come home and get money off my ability to hustle and that alone. Although I hadn't ruled it out as a backup plan, there was never supposed to be any robberies and there was definitely never supposed to be any hits for hire. I think the moment I'd stored those things away as a backup plan, I set a self-fulfilling prophecy in motion. My fears of poverty led to desperate decision making even when I wasn't in desperate times.

I had to take a step back. I started to spend more time at home again because it was the only time I felt at peace. My main spot was doing good, but my cost of living was rising, so I still didn't see myself moving in the direction of getting out of the game any time soon.

I began to hear whispers that Big Smoke had resurfaced in the hood again. Word on the street was he had been hanging around Crack Park with the smokers. One day, I went to one of my loyal customer's house to let him know that my shop was back open after being shut down for a couple of days. Big Smoke came to the door and opened it. I didn't see any fear in his eyes.

For a minute, I wondered did he even remember robbing me. I think he'd done so much dirt he could no longer keep up. I looked inside and saw there was a full house. I knew it wasn't the time or the place. I played it cool and asked for the house owner. Big Smoke said he wasn't there, and I went on

KING BENJAMIN

my way. I knew the next time I went to kill him, I had to finish the job. He wasn't worth all trouble I was going through, but my pride wouldn't let it go. After that, I started to see him on a regular basis, but each time, he wouldn't see me.

I'd ride by and he'd be right in front of Crack Park sitting in a van surrounded by addicts. I knew he carried a pistol, and I knew he probably realized that if not me, others were looking for him because of his grimy past.

Whenever I'd see him, he was always surrounded by too many people and I wouldn't be in a position to make a move. I patiently waited for the right opportunity to follow him out of the neighborhood and catch him at a stoplight and leave him there. I couldn't miss this time. I had to finish the job.

Each day that passed, I grew angrier that he was still alive and parading around the neighborhood like shit was sweet. Never once had I considered all the dirt I'd done and how things came back around. There was just no way we could coexist after what he'd done. I knew I'd never find the other two guys, so he had to be the one to die for it. I'd started selling a little weight by now, trying to establish clientele. Most of my days were spent handling business so each time I ran into him, that's when it would register that he was still alive.

One day a friend of mine that knew all about the robbery pulled up on me at the liquor store. He told me he knew exactly where Big Smoke lived. I told him to take me to his house, and he did just that. When we got there the van that Big Smoke drove wasn't there. He told me if the van was in the driveway that meant he was definitely inside. I thanked him for all his help and dropped him back off at home. This time, I wasn't leaving any part of this job in anybody else's hands. I was going on this ride solo to make sure it was done right.

I just knew this was going to be easy. Big Smoke was slowly starting to relax it seemed. Then, all of sudden, out of the blue, he started driving around with his girlfriend and a

FIGHT OF MY LIFE

newborn baby in the van with him. Every time I saw the van, I'd see the girl in the passenger seat. That meant following him out of the hood definitely wasn't an option. I only wanted Big Smoke, nobody else, and definitely no women and kids. I think the girl and the kid were an extra line of security for him. I wasn't the only one that wanted this nigga, but I was determined to catch him slipping first.

My throwaway nine came with some cheap copper-top bullets when I bought it off the streets. I threw those away and went and bought two boxes of hollow tips for Big Smoke and whoever else I could catch up with. I still wasn't sure if the information my homeboy had given me was legit, so I drove past the house before I went home and sure enough, there was the van in the driveway. I was so excited I could smell the death in the air. This meant I could catch Big Smoke away from the hood and keep my name completely out of it.

That night, I planned the hit out very carefully. I didn't want anything left to chance, so I addressed every precaution before I went to sleep. The next day, I arrived in the hood ready to do business as usual but that night, Big Smoke's ass was all mine. I knew I would have murder on my mind heavily all day, but I tried to bring a sense of normalcy to the day by making it as routine as possible. I bought some weed and went to the liquor store to get blunts. I drove to the spot to drop the work off to Jimmy, but he was nowhere to be found so I decided to open up myself.

After being at the spot for less than twenty minutes, traffic started flowing fast and heavy. A female that was a regular customer came in and stood in the middle of the floor waiting for me to serve her the drugs.

"You heard about Big Smoke?" she asked.

My antennas went up.

"No, what about 'em?" I asked, giving her my undivided attention.

"He had an asthma attack and died."

KING BENJAMIN

It registered slowly. She had to be joking.

"You lying!" I said with a more shock than intended in my tone.

"I swear," she replied and went on to say the whole hood was talking about it.

At first, I still couldn't believe it. People were rumored to be dead in the hood all the time and would pop up months later. Within the hour, more people came through the door with the same news, and it continued to be the big talk of the day. Honestly, my initial reaction was a bit of relief that I didn't have to kill anybody that night. But after I got some time alone to process things, I realized that what I'd just experienced had to be what they call divine intervention. What were the chances of a guy dropping dead of asthma the same day I had every intention of killing him?

For the first time in a long time, I realized God was watching. The feeling shook me to the core. It made me feel like I must have a purpose. It made me feel like for whatever reason, He cared about me. I started to feel like maybe my life wasn't meant to be spent in a prison cell wasting away or gunned down in my late twenties. It didn't change anything immediately but from that day, a seed was planted.

I turned all my attention to hustling and coming up as fast as I could so I could get out of the game. The thing that kept me motivated was that I knew how things could take off like a rocket at any given moment. If a drought came, I could make a quick hundred grand in a matter of months. I knew that wasn't a lot of money, but it would open the door for legitimate investments, and I'd be one step closer. I started to focus on my second house near the freeway, trying to get it up to a few thousand a day like the first house. I started passing out sacks to anybody that wanted to work. I was also working on opening up another house on Van Dyke. If I had three spots up and running, there was no way I could lose.

FIGHT OF MY LIFE

As the money started really flowing again, I got a little distracted by the women in my life. I started dating like I wasn't in a relationship already, spending money clubbing, restaurants, and shopping. These were things I always did on a regular, but not to the point where the money would be missed.

The worst part was I wasn't really doing anything with my girlfriend. I stopped coming home every night and used hustling as my excuse. She knew that was a lie. I was truly focused on getting out of the game, but I was also giving in to a lot of temptation. At this point, all I did was drop off drugs and pick up money, so there was no reason to be out all night. My goals were clear, but I was getting money and trying to enjoy it at the same time. One day, the guy that was working the second house ran off with all the drugs and the money.

It took a minute to find a replacement for him, so I had to close the spot temporarily. The second house was a real shit hole and nobody wanted to work it. Everybody wanted to work the first house, but I didn't need workers for that one. It became a challenge for me to work on opening a third spot because I was too busy trying to keep the second spot open. Eventually, the fiend that lived there told another dealer he could use the house until I was ready to open it back up. We put the dealer out without incident, but we beat the fiend up pretty bad for trying to play me. The dealer was an unknown and was making money from my customers, who would've never went there to buy drugs. It was his house but my spot.

When it was over, I thought about the fact that it was the first time I'd had to do harm to someone since before Big Smoke passed away. A lot of time had passed. Sounds crazy, but I realized at the moment I'd calmed down a lot. I didn't want my violent streak to return but sometimes, there was no way to hustle in the streets without it. Knowing a little about karma, it was always in the back of my mind to curve my animal instinct if the situation warranted it. The whole Big Smoke thing had brought my conscience back to the forefront and along with it a bit of apprehension.

KING BENJAMIN

I still carried a gun every day, but I began to hope I didn't have to use it. I finally got Jimmy to open the second spot back up, and I was thinking I would finally get a smooth run with both houses without something going wrong. I remember hearing about this white girl named Angel that was supposed to be snitching in the hood.

She came to my spot while I was there, and I told her she couldn't get served. She basically cursed me out and told me she would have my spot shut down. That was the first time I truly refrained myself from violence, because I really wanted to ram her head into a wall for threatening me that way and I didn't. Not long after that, I ran into the young boy from Van Dyke who had shot at me. I had my gun with me as I pulled into the same gas station where it all started with him hitting my car. He spotted me at the same time I spotted him.

I hopped out with my gun in my hand, but my body was concealed by the car as I tucked the gun in my back pocket. As we locked eyes, he froze and went to turn and walk back from the direction he'd came. I called out to him.

"Let me holla at you."

I could tell he wasn't strapped. I could see the mental conversation going on in his head by his body language as he gathered his nerves and then headed in my direction. I was positive he didn't have a gun because of his attempt to avoid me at first sight. The ball was completely in my court.

"What's up, you still wanna get busy?" I questioned, knowing the answer already.

"That shit dead, man," he replied humbly.

"You sure?" I asked him, getting closer.

"It's been dead as far as I'm concerned."

I could see the fear in his eyes. I knew had I seen this kid a few months earlier, I would've shot him without hesitation. He still owed me money for hitting my car. But I also knew at

FIGHT OF MY LIFE

this point I was being tested, and this test just might dictate how the rest of my life played out. I squashed it with the youngin' right then and there. If felt good to actually walk away from a beef for once. I didn't know it then, but this was only the beginning of many tests.

The following year would bring a series of events that would change my life forever. The game was still a rollercoaster ride with wins and losses. As more time passed, I eventually forget about being on the run for the dope case and violation of parole. I started driving like I was really out here legit, catching speeding tickets and traffic violations. My fake driver's license gave me a false sense of security, as if I was untouchable. Soon, it got suspended, and I stopped driving. After not driving for a couple of weeks, I ended up selling my car, which was a horrible idea.

It was too hard to get around every day with no car, so I started driving again using my girl's car but only for business runs. One day, the police followed me and Jimmy into a gas station and hit the lights and siren on me. I had two ounces of powered coke stashed in the car, plus we had just finished smoking weed. I looked around and there was absolutely nowhere to run. It happened so fast, I decided to play it cool and hand him my suspended license. When the cop took my license and paperwork, he headed back to the car. I took the dope out of the stash and gave it to Jimmy.

After I handed the dope over, I realized that the tags on my girl's car had expired the day before. I was supposed to be taking care of it that day. Even though there was nowhere to run, I told Jimmy to make a run for it if they asked us both to step out of the car. My heart was racing just knowing I could be about to return to prison with even more felony charges. The officer came back to the car and handed me a ticket for running a red light and told me to have a nice day. Believe or not, instead of being relieved, I actually sat behind the wheel trying to dispute the ticket.

KING BENJAMIN

I even took a couple cheap shots at him before it hit me that I could've been in handcuffs on my way back to prison. I quickly humbled myself. As I drove off, that's when it hit me that God slowly but surely was taking control of things. I knew it was a direct reflection of all the nights I'd been up praying that I was granted more time with my kids before I went away. I got pulled over again a month later with a suspended license, but my tags were legit so I decided to try my luck. Once again, I was ticketed with no mention of the suspended license and told to have a nice day. At the time, I couldn't fully understand why I was catching so many breaks, but I knew it was some type of divine intervention and at that point, I wasn't going to jail until it was my day to go. As I go over the edits for this book, it's now the year 2020 and police brutality in America is at the forefront of an uprising that has literally spread all across the globe. I will admit that those incidents back then let me know there were some decent cops that weren't out there just looking to lock up and beat the shit out of people instead of protecting and serving, it's just way too fucking many that are.

Months later, I was training a new worker on how to run the spot. I sat there with him and we smoked a blunt and drank some Hennessy as I introduced him to all of my loyal customers. After I made sure he knew the ropes, I poured another red cup of Hennessy and headed out to go home for the night. I sat the Hennessy in the cup holder and turned up Jeezy's "Thug Motivation." I remember feeling good about where I was financially at that moment. I had some new workers and money was flowing in good. I hit Chene Street headed to the freeway in a celebratory mood.

I spotted a police officer in the third lane, but he was nice enough to let me out in traffic in front of him, or so I thought. As soon as I pulled out in front of him, he flicked the lights to pull me over. I figured I hadn't done anything to warrant a traffic stop, but I was under the influence with a big cup of Hennessy in the car with me. I was sure the strong scent of

FIGHT OF MY LIFE

cognac was all over me and the car. I knew my chances of getting lucky this time were almost nonexistent. As I crawled closer to the red light, deciding if I was going to stop or not, he cruised right behind me. I told myself I wasn't going to jail this day. It didn't feel like my day and I wasn't ready.

Not while things were going so good, and definitely not before I had spent some more time with my kids. I made a turn down a one-way street the wrong way, knowing the officer may not want to risk his life on a simple traffic stop. I stomped the gas as I saw a clear lane, then shot across Warren to the first residential street. I hit Grandy and stomped the gas again. I drove up Grandy doing every bit of ninety miles an hour. I thanked God no one was on the road, because I could've surely killed myself or someone else.

Even after I realized I had lost the first squad car, I wouldn't slow down because I was sure he'd called for backup. I expected to look up and see five cars headed my way. I continued stomping the gas as the car lifted into the air with each hump in the raggedy road, until I was almost at the freeway. When I tried to slow down, I couldn't decrease my speed enough to make the complete turn.

The car spun out on the service drive and crashed into the guard rail surrounding the entrance ramp. I don't remember if the car was still running, but the bumper was stuck on the guard rail and I was in a ditch. There wasn't much damage done to the car, but I knew I didn't have time to get myself out of the ditch. I knew police were coming and probably headed right in my direction.

I hopped out and fled on foot, leaving the car behind. I ran up the block until I began to grow tired. I was injured, but my adrenaline was so high I was able to ignore the pain in my ribcage and left hand. I looked through a field and spotted the police on the next block. I sat on a stranger's porch as if I lived there while they drove to the scene of my crash. I sat on the porch for about twenty minutes. As they investigated, I took

KING BENJAMIN

inventory of the damage I'd done to myself. My knuckle was definitely broken, and I had at least a couple of fractured ribs. My girl called me, and I told her what happened and that I wouldn't be able to pick her up from work.

After she realized I'd crashed her car, I don't think she heard anything else after that. She was so upset about the car, I don't even know if she cared whether I made it home safe or not. I let enough time pass before I walked to a house that I knew I could sit and wait for a taxi at. I really didn't feel like going home and listening to my girl bitch about me leaving her car all night. I'd had a rough day, to say the least. Instead, I went and got drunk with some friends and replayed the dramatic event, trying to not think about how bad my ribcage hurt. I never went to the hospital, afraid that I would be identified and arrested.

After I got as high as I could get, I remember walking out to the porch for some fresh air as I contemplated the rollercoaster that was my life. It seemed like I was always in danger of something. I couldn't help but be thankful that I wasn't in jail, but I was really starting to wonder what the future held for me. I didn't feel like I had control of my life anymore but couldn't grasp the fact that God just really wanted me to change.

KARMA

I FINALLY WENT HOME TO face the music with my girl, and it was just as I expected it would be. A lot of screaming and hollering back and forth and no one listening to the other. I assured her I would buy her another car in a week or two, and I felt like that should've been the end of it. Realistically, her car was only worth a few grand, but I felt like the value of me being on the streets was limitless. She'd bought the car with her own money that she'd worked for and wasn't trying to hear it. I understood being pissed, but I felt she went way overboard.

Somehow, with all I had done for her, she didn't see how valuable I could be on the streets. I think that was the first time I realized how unappreciative she was, but it was only the beginning. When I finally went back to the main spot, the new worker was gone. The fact that it looked as if he'd left in a hurry left a bad taste in my mouth. The door was left unlocked, and he hadn't called or text me. I looked around inside to see if the police had torn up the house, but it was evident police hadn't been there. I stood there as the realization kicked in that this guy had ran off with my money.

I went to look for him, but he was nowhere to be found. I went to look for Jimmy to help me set up shop, but he was missing as well. By the time I came back to the hood the next day, the house owner said we needed to talk. He told me that police had been riding heavy and he felt like a raid was coming. I told him I would shut down for a couple weeks, but he had different ideas. He wanted to shut down permanently. Initially, when he agreed to rent me the house, it was a six-month deal. I had already been there over nine months, but we were both eating good from my stay, so I figured I had more time. But what could I do? If he didn't want to go on, I had to shut it down, but I figured he just needed some time to cool off and stop being nervous.

After that disappointing day, I decided I needed to stay home and heal for a few days. When I tried that, all my girl wanted to do was argue about her car and anything else she could think of. I was supposed to be putting the money together to buy her a car, but now I was taking losses and I didn't have my money spot to help me recover. The fighting got so bad between us I just packed up my clothes and left for a few weeks. During this time, I wasn't making much money, just spending it on everyday life.

After some time, I caught up with Jimmy and gave him the work to sell at the other house by the freeway. He worked a few days and went missing again. Jimmy had always been a good friend of mine so I wasn't too worried, but I needed the money. Things were going so bad I had to think about the possibility that I wouldn't find Jimmy. Luckily, when I finally did catch up with him, he had all the money, but he didn't want to work the house by the freeway anymore.

The fact that he had went in hiding instead of just telling me the truth made me feel like it was probably time we cut our business ties to save the friendship. Things were going downhill fast and hard. Without Jimmy, I had no help to push my work on the block. That left me to do it all on my own again and at that point, I realized I couldn't really afford to hire anyone else to help me if I wanted to. Once I had to sit in the house by the freeway, I understood why nobody wanted to work there. The house was a really nasty and so was the fiend that lived there. I could've just put him out and took over the

FIGHT OF MY LIFE

house myself, but he was a good handyman and the house always needed something fixed.

The freeway house was making money but nowhere near enough to compensate for the house I'd shut down. After a few weeks, I moved back in with my girl, thinking we were on the same page again, only to experience the same constant feuding nonstop. I thought she'd consider all my circumstances, but all she cared about was me replacing her car. I moved out again and came back a month later. I was still in love with her, but I was moving back in for convenience more than anything. I'd already figured out we weren't going to last, but I tried to ride it out. Business was going slower every day and I couldn't understand why.

I had the best product, and I was still giving out the same quantity. That was my formula and it always worked until now. I contemplated getting my own place, but I wasn't ready to leave my kids. I was so stressed out I remember drinking every day to cope. My kids were the only thing bringing me joy at that point. But things never improved between me and her. It came to a point I knew what I had to do. Even though my name was on the lease, and most of the bills were in my name, and I owned half of everything in the house, I knew I had to leave.

I couldn't ask her to move when I knew she had the kids, so there was no other choice available. I told myself I'd started looking for a house but the day after I said that, the freeway house got raided. The fiend was the only one in the house at the time. He went to jail for a syringe and some old warrants. This forced me to stay home, even though my girl and I couldn't stand one another. I couldn't move with no income.

I couldn't afford to sell weight anymore, so I just sat at home with a bunch of drugs and nowhere to sell them. I felt like the walls were closing in more each day. Hoping to create some peace, I finally offered to buy my girl another car while I still had enough money to do so. It wasn't much but it figured

KING BENJAMIN

it beat being without a car. She wasn't satisfied at all, but I told her if she wanted the bills paid, she needed to take what I could afford. At this point, had I not been on the run, I would've been better off going to look for a job, but I couldn't. I was a fugitive with parole violations and a new drug charge.

Around two weeks after the house got raided, I went back to it, hoping I could salvage whatever clientele I still had. I didn't get thirty days in before they raided it again. I walked up to the back porch and saw that the door had been kicked in. I was just about at the end of my rope. I really just wanted to say fuck hustling! I'm retired.

I walked to the nearest smoke house just trying to clear my head. I couldn't understand what was happening to my life. I felt like my gut was trying to give me the heads up that this part of my life was over. Maybe I'd made all the money I was ever going to make selling drugs. I told myself if I didn't find a new spot to hustle soon, I was out the game. When I got to the smoke house, I told the owners what happened and they told me I could sit there and catch my customers for a few days.

A few days turned into a few weeks, and then so much for being out of the game. My brother came home on parole and I felt like since he went to jail hustling for me, I owed him. I bought him some clothes and gave him a place to stay while he figured things out. My girl tried to act like she was okay with my brother living there, but I knew she didn't like it. Shit, I don't even know if she was okay with me being there at the time. So I took him with me every time I left the house. Eventually, I saw he wasn't trying to get a job, so that only left him one option.

I let him sit around the new spot and become familiar with the faces. I had to feed him and support all his habits during this time, and I knew that wasn't something that could last. My girl was becoming irritated that my brother was there, so we began to argue again almost every day. I tried to give my brother a bag and let him run the spot but instead, he got drunk

FIGHT OF MY LIFE

and cursed all the customers out. Then he'd lay down and go to sleep for the night and the next day, I'd hear about all the customers who weren't getting served.

Soon, it finally hit me that I was suffering from all the bad karma I'd created throughout the years. All the things I'd done were coming back on me in the worst way because the most painful state for me had always been the financial struggle. The house was doing okay, but somehow I was still sinking like my feet were in quicksand. I told my brother things weren't working out and that I would give him something to go out and hustle on his own terms. When I did, he fucked up the money I gave him pretty fast, but I couldn't hold his hand any longer.

As soon as things started to pick up a little, I went back to creeping with other girls to keep my mind off my problems. By now I wasn't in love anymore, but I wasn't ready to leave. One day my girl drove right by me with another girl in the car. I knew she saw me, and I tried to lie my way out of it, but it was pointless. About a week later, I drove by her and spotted a guy in her passenger seat. I turned around and followed her to the next light. When she finally pulled over to let him out on a block we were both familiar with, she claimed that the guy was doing some work on her car. I knew it was lie because she'd been ignoring my phone calls while they were together.

It was all I needed to come to grips with the fact our relationship was truly over. I moved out of the house for good. In the end, I realized I'd never spent enough time with her to keep her happy. I always thought paying the bills was enough, but it turned out she needed me there more than anything. I was a good father, but I wasn't a good boyfriend.

I began to pray every night for answers while I looked for a place to live. I just didn't know what to do with my life, so I kept hustling, trying to turn things around. My brother came back around when I was trying to take a trip to New York. I gave him a second chance to run the spot so I could leave

KING BENJAMIN

town, and he fucked me. The minute he thought that I was gone, he took off and went missing with the money, my gun, and the drugs. When I found out, I wasn't even surprised. He was still holding a grudge about the weed house. I just remember thinking if it wasn't for bad luck, I wouldn't have any.

OUT THE DOPE GAME

I REALLY NEEDED TO GET away for a minute, so the New York trip was right on time. I got a chance to leave all of my problems behind and spend money on things that mattered to me. My sisters were there, and I felt like they were the only people I had in my corner. While I was New York, I realized how much of life I was missing out on always in the hood hustling. There was so much more to life than the street shit I'd been on.

I thought about God on a regular and I could feel myself being guided toward Him. I knew He would help me out of my situation if I prayed hard enough and really tried to change my life. I didn't know what would be the first step in the direction of change, but I knew I was tired of selling crack. When I came back from New York, I prayed harder than I ever had in my life. I had to turn things around because I still had kids to raise. I prayed for God to take control of my life and give me some type of direction. I wasn't ready to be born again or nothing, but I was ready to leave the street life behind me.

I still had to sell drugs because I had no work experience, and I was on the run. At first it felt like I was just trapped in the game. I realized I could just turn myself in and deal with the situation, but that was about as realistic as me becoming an R&B singer. I loved my kids way too much to willingly leave them for only God knows how long. Besides that, I'd been to prison twice, so I knew exactly what was waiting for me, and I would've never offered myself up to that type of retribution.

KING BENJAMIN

I found a house to move into, but it wasn't quite ready yet. During this time, I was living with my sister, but we were growing annoyed with each other just because it's difficult to live with anyone when you're used to having your own. I didn't want to be a burden to anyone, so I bounced around to homies' houses until my house was ready. Once I moved into my new home, I felt like it was a new beginning. Just as I was at the end of my rope, things were starting to get better. I continued to pray nightly for everything I wanted. Learning how to leave it all in God's hands released a great amount of stress I'd been carrying around. It was amazing that even though I'd done all these ruthless things, He was still right there waiting on me with open arms. I could feel His presence working in my life on a daily just by little things that were happening. I still didn't have anything, but suddenly I was at peace and I was happy.

One day a female customer that was causing confusion at the spot sent the police there, saying we had kidnapped someone. Luckily, I left when she made the threat about calling the police, but the fact that I didn't try to retaliate made me know that I was truly changing for the better. At the same time, I had to ask myself was I going soft because I was letting crack heads pick on me and get away with snitching. I still didn't have a plan to exit the game, but I knew it was time. If I wasn't going to be a drug kingpin, then what was I going to do? I didn't understand God's plan at all, but at least I wasn't stressed.

I knew I wasn't going to be a rapper, and it didn't look like I was going to be a drug kingpin either. So just what the hell was I going to do with the rest of my life? I was almost thirty years old now and still hadn't found my purpose. I started to visit Barnes and Noble a lot because I stopped smoking weed and now, I needed something to do to pass the time while I was selling drugs. I bought *Confessions of a Video Vixen* by Karrine Steffans and *Never Go Home Again* by Shannon Holmes. When I finished reading the book by Shannon Holmes, I read the about the author bio in the back of the

FIGHT OF MY LIFE

book. I gathered from the bio that Shannon Holmes had lived the street life and had also been to prison.

An unexplainable feeling came over me. I didn't know it was the answer to my prayers, I just knew something hit me like a brick in the head. I remembered that English was always my strong point in school. I remembered how I'd always had an interest in expanding my vocabulary my whole life. I'd learned to type in prison, which was a skill I thought I'd never actually need. It was all coming to me so fast. This had to be it! This had to be my ticket out of the streets. Staring at Shannon Holmes' face in the bio pic, I just knew that someone who had been through similar circumstances had done it already.

I think that gave me all the motivation I needed just to know that someone else was already doing it. I didn't matter if it took me ten years to accomplish this goal I was about to set for myself. Being a 40-year-old writer sounded much better than being a 35-year-old rapper. I always like to sleep on something before I make a final decision, but when I went to sleep and woke up the next day, I still had the same powerful feeling that this was my calling.

Somehow, I was going to become a writer of urban fiction novels. I'd lived enough life in the streets to never run out of stories. Even though it was just an idea, it was the best feeling in the world. I had a plan. I had a passion. Everything I'd seen and lived would be stirred into my life's work and spilled out on these pages, forever cementing my place in history. I didn't know the first thing about writing or storytelling, but I came up with an idea for my first book, so I started writing about a week later.

My sense of purpose grew stronger every day. I hustled on the weekdays, and on the weekends, I'd have my kids over and spend time with them. I cherished every moment of those weekends because I knew that one day, I would have to face the music. From that point on, all I did was write, hustle, and spend time with my kids. Nothing else was important. My ex was having money problems after I left, so she tried to rekindle what we had, but the love was gone. I gave her money for what the kids needed but nothing more.

I continued to pray for guidance. Sometimes I'd have a bad week financially and thoughts of robbery would resurface, but I would just pray and keep going. When things got real tight, I started selling my guns to remove the temptation of going out robbing. As always, eventually, my last drug house started getting enough traffic to attract the police and get on their radar. As I saw my traffic constantly increasing, it made me nervous about the possibility of catching another dope case to add on to the one I already had.

I started drinking and smoking again, because I would be paranoid sitting in the house, knowing I could get raided any day. Another case meant more years in prison. One day I was rolling a blunt and I let a customer in that had a strange look in his eyes.

"What's up?" I asked.

"Police parked down the street watching the house," he informed me.

I took off to go and stash my dope. When I came back, I went outside and looked around, but I didn't see any sign of the police. I went back inside and finished rolling up my blunt, but I kept my dope in the stash. As I put the blunt to my mouth to light it, I heard police yelling and kicking on the door. The back door was barricaded and there was no way to quickly escape. I ran upstairs just to get as far away from the dope as possible. It was a huge house, so I was hoping I'd find somewhere to hide.

But once I heard the police running through the house, I decided not to hide. I was pretty confident they wouldn't find anything. When I heard the officers coming up the stairs, I put my hands up and surrendered peacefully. The first officer I

FIGHT OF MY LIFE

came in contact with roughed me up a little then threw the cuffs on me. He searched me for drugs and didn't find any. When they took me downstairs, I realized I was the only one in handcuffs. When I asked why, he told me to shut the fuck up, and I did.

As I looked at two of the officers that were in the house, I realized they were the same narcs that arrested me two years ago at the garage. As they made us all lay down, I thought to myself, well, this is it. It's all over. It was obvious that I was the dealer and everyone else in the house was a user. But when they asked me why I was there, I told them I had a prostitute upstairs, but she'd left before they came. They didn't buy it. They snatched me up and took me to the police car to run my name. When they started to run my name, I realized they didn't recognize me. The name on my fake identification had no warrants and they didn't find any drugs. They took the cuffs off me and let me go.

By this time, I was so in tune with what God was trying to show me I understood that I was only still on the streets because of my commitment to changing my life. I was only being given time to find my path and spend time with the people I loved. It was all I prayed for and my wish was being granted. I had already secured my next crack house even before the raid. By now, I knew every house I got was on a timer, and I could smell a raid a mile away most of the time. I tried transferring the customers again, but a lot of people didn't make the transition. My very last crack house was real fucked up, like the one by the freeway.

It was hard for me to sit there for hours on end just to make the measly profits I made with each flip. I had to keep going just to pay my bills. I was always happy at home trying to write or just relaxing, but as soon as I had to go hustle, I immediately grew depressed about the whole situation. I told God that whenever He saw fit for me to leave the streets, I would now be willing to go do my time. I knew once I was off the streets I would be out of the dope game, and I'd spend my

KING BENJAMIN

time working on my writing skills. During my last days on the run, I came across a 40-caliber pistol that I purchased for next to nothing. I only bought it because it was too good of a deal to pass up.

As soon as I had another gun in possession, thoughts of robbery resurfaced, but I knew that was only the devil trying to throw me off track. I know it sounds crazy to say I was committed to change yet I continued to sell drugs, but I had to take baby steps. I was still in a state of confusion and I knew the change would be a slow process. I had been a criminal for almost fifteen years, so it was literally all I knew. I knew I had to hustle or be evicted, so I did what made sense at the time. I remember listening to DMX's "Lord Give Me a Sign" almost every day my last days as a crack dealer. In the end, I was truly sick and tired of the streets.

On September 23, 2006, the day before my weekend visit with the kids, I was stopped by police while walking down the street. They said I looked suspicious dressed in all black, so they randomly stopped me. They found a small amount of drugs on me and I was arrested. I didn't even think to run or try to hide the drugs. I was tired and ready to face whatever was going to happen to me. I was finally out of the game.

CHANGE GON' COME

I REALLY DIDN'T FEEL THE way a person usually feels when he gets arrested. I didn't feel like the world was coming to an end. Even though I was facing two new charges, a huge weight had been lifted from my shoulders. I rode to the station at peace, ready to get it over and done with. To me, this was the end of an era and the beginning of a new life. The only time I got down was when I realized that I was about to leave my kids. That thought brought tears to my eyes. My daughter was only 18 months old.

Although I knew I had to deal with my past one day, nothing can really prepare you for going to prison a third time. The police came to me and tried to offer me a way out of my situation. Detroit had been the murder capital off and on for the past five or six years, and this seemed to be one of the years we were striving to get back to the top.

The police offered to drop both the drug charges in exchange for a tip on some gun dealers. I knew plenty of people to call if I needed artillery, but I had a code that I lived by. A code that was said to be extinct, but I couldn't let that part of me die. I was always the type of person who would do a hundred years before I told on another man, and no amount of circumstances would change that. But I was a rare breed nowadays, and I knew that. It was part of the reason I knew it was time for me to say goodbye.

The fact that nobody was respecting the game was sickening to me. I realized that by the time I made it to the level of success I was striving for, someone was going to either

KING BENJAMIN

rob and kill me or snitch on me. It's just the way the game was now. Maybe it was the way it always was, but I knew I had to accept it or get out. Between all the shady plugs selling stepped-on dope and all the backstabbing that always came with the game, it just wasn't worth it any longer. I got out, but I left with my street morals and integrity intact. I told them I didn't know anything about anything, and I wanted to go to my cell and lay down. After a few days, my case was brought over from 36 District Court to Frank Murphy Hall of Justice, and I was sent to the county jail.

Each time I was placed in the county jail I thought the same thing. This was the foulest, most disgusting, depressing place on earth. Just the thought of having to go through county to get to prison was enough to stay on the run forever. It was so overcrowded at the time, I had to sleep on the floor in the gym the first couple of nights I was there. From there, I went to quarantine where all everyone did all day was play cards and Dominoes.

Both games usually led to a fight. Everybody rushed the doors when the food came like savages. You had to be that way or there was a chance you'd end up fighting for your own food. Once I got to a rock, I thought things would be different, but it wasn't. The only difference was the two main rooms.

Guys still rushed the door for food like they weren't going to feed everybody, and they still fought about card games on a regular. The county deputies treated the inmates like shit and talked to them like they were scum. I never said anything to them unless I absolutely had to. There was a girl I knew from the streets that was a county deputy, but I was never able to get close enough to her workstation to let her know I was there.

Going to court was the worst part of it all. Waking up at 3 am and sitting in cell after cell with funky inmates all day. I would stand at the front of the cell trying to breath in enough outside air to keep from passing out. Shackled and cuffed, I'd

FIGHT OF MY LIFE

be tossed in a van and driven through the underground tunnel that led back to the courthouse. As I arrived at the courthouse, I told myself I'd never go through this shit again. No amount of money was worth what I had put myself through in the last ten years. When I came back from court, I hadn't eaten anything but some cereal at 5AM and a bologna sandwich at 11.

I had missed lunch and dinner wasn't even enough food to feed my daughter. I laid on my bunk that night feeling like I was about to starve to death. All the money I had in my pockets when arrested was confiscated as drug money. I hadn't been there long enough for any money I was sent to process, so there was literally nothing I could do and no one to blame. I knew this was the beginning of another rough journey. I was no longer the hustler that always found a way to make it happen. I didn't even have a name in here. I was just another number. I was nobody.

Even when I told the people in charge that my name wasn't spelled right on my jail ID, they'd say "it doesn't matter, we got your number." I was literally just a number here. I knew deep down I was more than a jailbird with a number instead of a name, but what I saw and what they saw were two completely different things. I just knew I couldn't let the reality of my situation get the best of me. I had to be strong and keep my mind intact in the midst of the storm. Sometimes I would start to think maybe God didn't have a plan for me after all but each time, I would shake off that thought. But the longer I sat, that doubt continued to try and creep in.

I prayed for answers and kept the faith that this was all a part of the process of turning my life around and heading in a new and positive direction. As I'd promised myself, once I was incarcerated, I buried myself into writing. I was spending whole days just writing, which left me with no down time to think negative or feel sorry for myself. At night I prayed for guidance then left it all in God's hands. On my second court date I was offered a plea for six months to twenty years. I was

KING BENJAMIN

flabbergasted. I immediately felt my life changing for the better right there in that courtroom.

I had two dope cases plus a parole violation. I took the plea before the court-appointed attorney could even finish explaining the details. Even if the parole board decided to give me another year, that only gave me 18 months total. I never expected to be offered such a low plea. To this day, I still don't fully understand it, I just know God was on my side. I was expecting two years at the minimum and maybe another year or two from the parole board. That would've been a total of ten years in prison bids I'd racked up when it was over. Now I could see the light and I believed more than ever that I had a future worth saving. I believe once again that God was showing me that He was with me for whatever reason.

By the time I went to Jackson, I had my mind made up that my life had purpose and nothing that I was about to go through even mattered. With everything I had been through in the past year, prison started to feel like a welcomed vacation. I didn't go outside at all the 45 days I was in Jackson. I sat in my cell and wrote *Respect My Gangsta*, which later became *The War Report*. Nothing about the situation could really get to me. The disrespectful COs or the grimy, cutthroat inmates. I never got lonely, I never got bored, and I never got homesick. I should've been miserable, but I felt like the worst was over and I was about to turn my whole life around.

There were five tiers on each side and approximately five hundred inmates inside 7 block. Nobody would consider this environment peaceful. All the inmates did all day was yell back and forth across the gallery, but here I was at total peace like I was in the Bahamas. I would come to eat or shower and go back to my cell and write. A lot had changed since the last time I'd visited Jackson. The food portions were skimpy as shit, and it reminded me of being in county all over again. But I was in such good spirits during this time, nothing bothered me. The good thing was that now we were allowed to order a few junk

FIGHT OF MY LIFE

food items from the store, and I had money in my account so I did just that.

While I was there, I ran into a guy I had done a couple years with on a previous bid. He was one of those dudes that liked to keep up with the Joneses, as they say. Always flossing like he was rich. He was the kind of guy that would call you a bum if you bought the 500 hundred Benz instead of the 600, even though he'd never had either. To support his lifestyle, he would rob any and everyone. We both had plans to get back to the street life when we were released from jail. And here we were, both back on our way to prison. But there was a big difference in the road that lied ahead for us. I had six months, and he had twenty-six years.

He lied about what the time was for, but I found out later he had robbed a hair salon and shot someone. He was sentenced as an habitual criminal for all his robbery and gun charges. But while I was standing there talking to him, I couldn't help but count my blessings. I knew that his situation could've easily been mine. I'd never robbed any hair salons, but I'd definitely done my share of dirt. By the time I was fed up with Jackson, they rode me out to the prison that I would do the remainder of my time at.

I was sent to a level-one prison, and I immediately set up a schedule to keep myself busy, which included finishing my first book. Once I landed back in prison, everything I needed to be a writer started falling in place. A guy I knew had a bunch of *Writer's Digest* magazines he'd stolen from another prison library. He had no real use for them, so he gave them all to me. Those books helped me sharpen my skills a lot. I would find books in the library that were directly in line with what I was trying to do or that related to my struggle at the time. I read Joyce Meyer's *Battlefield of the Mind* and Nathan McCall's *Makes Me Wanna Holler*. Those books were extremely helpful and I would still highly recommend them. I felt like God was guiding my every move.

KING BENJAMIN

Suddenly, it all made sense to me. One day, I looked around and all I could see was a bunch of suckas including myself. Almost everyone around me was on their second or third prison bid. Everyone thought they were so slick and had a master plan to get rich, and here we all were, and nobody was rich. It really pissed me off when I realized I'd fallen into the traps that had been laid out for black men in America through oppressive environments, lack of opportunity, and hopelessness. Unlike a lot of those I was surrounded by, I was finally tired enough to smarten up.

I wouldn't be back again, because I was foolish enough to still believe I would beat the odds on the lifespan of a crack dealer. My kids would not grow up being raised by another man, because I would grow up and learn another way to hustle. I understood now what my real definition of a man was, and it definitely wasn't a nigga that was so selfish they would continue to repeat the same cycle, risking the opportunity to raise what he created just to shine. I know that definitely doesn't define every street hustler's mentality, but it definitely defines way too many, especially nowadays. After some lengthy conversations, I'd come to realize none of the guys I was surrounded by were willing to sacrifice their material fetishes for the sake of their children.

By the time I started my second book, I could see improvement in my writing. Even though my first book was still a very rough draft, I knew it needed a lot of work. Before I knew it, the time came for me to see the parole board. I was very realistic about my chances after being on the run for two of the four years I'd been out of prison. But things were going so good, I figured I wouldn't count myself out. When the day came, I spoke to the parole board with confidence. In my eyes, I came off articulate and charming. I even got a few laughs out the parole board member that reminded me of Santa Claus. I knew I had his vote when I left the room. All I needed was one more from another member.

FIGHT OF MY LIFE

Unfortunately, I didn't get the second vote I needed to get the parole. My six months was now officially 18 months. I was disappointed after getting my hopes up after a good interview, but I kept it moving. I thought about the dude that had 26 years, and that really put things in perspective for me. I was fighting for a lot of things, but the most important was my freedom. I came up with a grueling workout routine then found some levelheaded dudes to kick the shit with and I did my time.

Once I made a firm decision to change my life, I decided I needed to recreate myself. It wasn't going to be easy, but I was going to give it everything I had. I'd been a street nigga for 15 years and I carried myself a certain way because of it. But now I needed to change the people around me. Most of the people I came in contact with on the streets on a daily basis were gangsters, hustlers, and addicts. If I wanted to get to the top of anybody's bestseller's list, I needed to change my circles and surroundings. In making this transition, the first thing I did was change my conversation. I stopped hanging on the yard with guys that only wanted to talk about drug houses and shootouts.

If a conversation headed in that direction, I'd just change the subject or I dipped out back to my unit. It wasn't going to help my cause to spend my days reminiscing on the past. The only time I really wanted to think about the street life was when I was writing about it. I had to reprogram myself. I knew I would always be a hood nigga. That would never change, but I had to remove the temptation of the game from my thought process. I knew what I was trying to accomplish was going to take a lot of patience, a lot of grind, and a lot of hustle. I knew it was going to take some balls to walk away from the very thing I had used to support myself my entire life.

I was about to try and enter a career field I knew nothing about. I was going to have to enter the working world for the first time. If anyone that did time with me during that eighteen months even remembered me, they'd probably say I was just a

KING BENJAMIN

quiet dude that stayed to myself and went to the library and the gym every day. I was prepping myself for what was to come. I read a lot street fiction writers that were hot at the time. Although the books were much more well written than mine, I felt like I had something original to offer the game.

The books I read by Terry Woods turned out to be my favorite. I was disappointed to learn she didn't write a lot of them. Still, I knew that she was self-published, and she really inspired me to want my own publishing company. But that was years away. Right now, I just wanted to become a bestselling writer. I had to think of a writer's name that sounded like it would catch the reader's attention. I came up the pen name King Benjamin for two reasons. I wanted to be the best in the game, so I crowned myself king ahead of time. The name Benjamin was just a way to keep something from my past. Benjamin Segal was the gangster I borrowed the nickname Bugsy from and used on the streets. Although he was rumored to hate that moniker, I loved it. Before long, Bugsy turned to Bug, which a lot of people still know me by to this day.

As time went on, things eventually got harder. The people that loved me began to keep in contact less and less. I found myself constantly having motivational conversations with myself. I knew that I was bigger than this jail shit, I just needed to get out. Soon, some guys I knew from the streets rode in and I found myself going down memory lane about the streets. I realized I would never be able to completely distance myself from my past nor did I want to. It was good for me to keep the pulse of the streets running through me as I was sharpening my skillset and crafting my own skill of urban fiction.

I realized I would always have ties to the streets, but that didn't mean I would be in them. The streets had made me who I was, and it was only because of the streets that I was able to pen these factionary tales so vividly. If I came up, I didn't want to be that dude that never went back to where he was from.

FIGHT OF MY LIFE

That dude that wanted to act like he was better than everybody else because he decided to change. Nah, that couldn't be me.

I also didn't want to be the dude that had everything and then lost it all trying to keep it real with niggas that didn't really care if he lived or died. I had to find a balance and separate my friends from my associates. My friends would understand what I was trying to accomplish, and anyone else didn't really matter. After being off the streets for a year, things got really tight for me financially. It seemed like everything was going wrong with everyone on the outside, which made things worse for me on the inside.

My pride wouldn't let me reach out to too many people because I felt like everyone had already shown me enough love during my previous bids. It was just a time that I had to man up and stand on my own two feet. Every day was one disappointment after the next. When I was waiting for some money to touch down, it made me realize how helpless I was at that time. I hated that feeling and never wanted to experience it again.

I can remember a month before it was time for me to see the board again, I would wake up early every morning and walk the track to clear my head. On the streets when things got bad, I could just go out and rob somebody to change my situation. Even in jail I'm sure I could've found somebody to rob, but I was supposed to be turning a new leaf. I'd never been this helpless for this long, and it was unexplainably uncomfortable. Not only was I broke, it was obvious that I was broke. In prison, you couldn't keep your fronts up. If you didn't have anything, it was gonna show.

Sometimes I woke up feeling like I was a complete failure and my whole life was a lie. I'd risked it all and had nothing to show for it. The devil was kicking me while I was down. It didn't matter that I had been making money since the age of sixteen, I didn't have any right now, and right now was all that mattered. It was around this time that I started watching TD

KING BENJAMIN

Jakes' *Potter's House* in the morning. That show helped me get through it. One of the biggest messages that reached me was about change. TD Jakes went on to say that God sometimes put people in situations where you have no choice but to trust Him. That's exactly where I was at.

Deep down inside, I just knew I would get my parole this time, and soon it would all be a distant memory. No more COs, no more chow halls and bullshit prison conversations. I don't want to get too religious, but I just want to point out that at this time, all I had was my faith in God. It was around this time that I came across a book called *The Secret*. It was all about the Law of Attraction. I was reading the book and watched the DVD during one of the programs I was in. It all just made so much sense to me.

I had already experienced the Law of Attraction in my life in so many ways, positive and negative. I started to study the law and tried using it to my advantage. I started telling everyone that would listen I was going home when I saw the parole board. I began to envision everything in my life in the future the way I wanted it to happen.

For some time, I could see the small benefits of my work, but nothing major. I remember how the book said don't give up if things don't happen all at once. My biggest thing on my wish list was my parole. The odds were stacked against me. A violent offender, with a parole violation and a new charge. There was no reason for them to be in a rush to let me go. I still continued to tell everyone I was coming home. Part of it was me telling God that I believed what He was placing in my heart to be truth. My heart and my gut were saying "you're going home."

Around Christmas time was when things started to happen. My finances started to improve quickly. Then the parole board came, and the interview went really well. Right before Christmas I was granted my parole, but that wasn't even the best part. I was granted a parole and enrolled into the re-

FIGHT OF MY LIFE

entry program, which basically meant I would have a couple months knocked off the remainder of the four months I had left. I would also be sent to Detroit to do the rest of my time.

Things continued to fall in place from there. I realized how real the Law of Attraction was and how important faith would be in my life moving forward. Once again, I vowed to never sell crack or rob again. I had two months left on my sentence, and I'd be going home to start my new life.

A NEW BEGINNING

I WAS RELEASED FROM PRISON the third and final time on February 26, 2008. I moved in with my sister for umpteenth time, and she welcomed me with open arms just like every other time. I got the same love and support from my family that I always got, but I knew I couldn't let them down again. The thing about going to jail is when you get out, it's like you're starting all over again if you get out broke. I was tired of starting over, and I vowed to never do it again.

The one thing I prayed about when I got out was finding a job. I knew that would have huge impact on my mental state and my ability to stay positive. There was always something about being broke that drove me to a place I just couldn't handle. I hated that feeling, and I hated the way people changed up when they knew you were struggling. I believed that God was guiding my steps going forward, so I was extremely optimistic. I'd been this positive before and ended up on the run in two weeks, but this time I had good intentions and a Higher Power backing my every move.

I knew a lot of dudes that had come home with good intentions but grew quickly frustrated because they just simply couldn't find employment. I was used to being my own man and I knew I couldn't allow myself to depend on my family for more than a month or two. I didn't even want to give myself time to wonder what would happen if things didn't go as planned after that. I put all my faith in God, and I just trusted that He would guide me in the right direction. I still remember the first time I saw my kids the day I got out.

FIGHT OF MY LIFE

I don't believe my daughter actually remembered me by face, but she pretended to be excited, jumping up and down because that's what my son was doing. It was such a wonderful feeling to be able to hold them again and kiss my little girl on the cheek. For the first few weeks I spent time with my kids and a girl that used to write me from time to time while I was away. I was still lining up all the job leads I could find while I got all of my identification in order. I planned to knock on every door I could until someone hired me.

But I was still in the space where things were just falling into my lap, so I didn't wind up knocking on any doors. By the time I got my identification in order, about two days later, I had a job. The same friend that rented me a house to sell dope out of for almost a year was now a supervisor at his job. Let's call this friend Terry. Terry would play a major role in my life going forward. The pay was lousy, but the job wasn't bad at all. It was pretty simple, just stuffing cloth in a box and sending it down a line.

As I got settled into a working schedule, there was one other thing that came as a plus this job had to offer. I met the most beautiful woman I'd ever known up to that point. I knew I wanted her the day I first laid eyes on her. I had nothing to offer anyone besides my friendship, but I was so drawn to her I knew we would connect sooner than later. After I got the job, my main focus was a vehicle. I got a ride to work most days, but I had to catch the bus home a lot of times. Catching the bus was the most humbling experience coming from the life. I hadn't seen the inside of a bus since I was a teenager. Standing at the bus stop hoping I didn't get spotted by someone that knew me as hustler, their boss, or even their enemy was rough. I knew I had to save every penny to get a whip.

I did take pride in the fact that as a man, I was willing to do whatever it took to stay out of prison and be a father to my children. It took me almost six months to save up for a car that I was comfortable with. It wasn't anything major, but it was clean, and it was mine. It was a burgundy Buick Oldsmobile

KING BENJAMIN

with a sunroof and leather interior. By now I had made friends with the girl that I wanted to get to know so bad. Her name was Marie and for a time, she was all I could think about. I really appreciated the fact that she accepted me for who I was. A man fresh out of jail with nothing to offer but friendship.

Once I had a car, I asked her on a date and she agreed. We went out to a nice restaurant and after that, we got a room nearby. This would be the start of another very special relationship for years to come. Marie was a big part of my life, and I remember waking up every day just looking forward to seeing her. In the beginning, we talked all day at work and even after we went home.

Now that I had a car, it was time for me to get out of my sister's house as fast as I could. But as the winter months kicked in, the hours at the job got cut. I started selling bootlegs DVDs at work to make up for the lost hours. I began to help my sister and my children's mother out as much as I could, but it didn't leave me with much money to consider saving. I knew this job didn't pay much, but I was slowly coming to a standstill with Christmas approaching.

I have to point out that, although I didn't have a lot of money, this was actually a very happy time in my life. I was alive, I was free, and I was exploring the next chapter of my life without any expectations. I was having a lot of fun on the social scene and hanging out, but the money just wasn't there. I really wanted to tighten my belt to make sure my kids had a good Christmas. I also realized I need to get back to writing and getting my books ready for print. It was easy to get distracted away from my goal to be a writer once I had all these real-life circumstances going on.

One day, right before Christmas, I walked into the job and they announced they were cutting the hours even more. We were down to five hours a day and it would be that way until after the New Year. I never even considered looking for some other part-time work because I was comfortable with the job I

FIGHT OF MY LIFE

had. I didn't have the best attitude when it came to authority and I knew I needed to be somewhere that I was comfortable and didn't feel like a slave. My friend was the supervisor. This was where I needed to be. So I toughed it out, but it was really bothering me to know I wasn't any closer to moving out of my sister's house.

Around the New Year, I realized that things weren't going to go back to normal as quick as they promised. By now, I was downright fed up, and the DVD money wasn't enough to make up for the lost hours. I knew a way that I could make more money while I was on the clock, but it involved a little risk. I'd been out a year now without making any bad decisions, but this one was really a no brainer. I already knew that half the people at my job smoked weed on their lunch breaks. I also knew that most of them bought the weed from guys at the job.

The problem was, nobody was making enough money to keep being a consistent supplier of weed. See, the thing was, most of the people that bought the weed ran up a credit tab and paid for it on pay day. That worked out good for the seller because you knew the money would be there. So, after I kept hearing that nobody in the plant had weed and people were constantly looking for it, I made a decision. I wish I could say I was completely hustle free after I came home, but that would be a lie. I'd made a promise to stop selling crack and robbing. I kept that promise; however, weed was a whole other story.

Honestly, I felt like I'd found a loophole in my plans and promises I'd made to myself, and God for that matter. I literally told myself that. I saw the money opportunity staring me in the face and I just had to take it. If I was going to stay at this dead-end job any longer, I knew it was time to make the most of it. I bought a half pound of weed and took over the small plant with the same formula I used to sell crack. I kept the best quality and quantity for the money they had to spend. When payday came, it was like I would pick up two checks instead of one. This would be my ticket out of my sister's house.

KING BENJAMIN

The next month I bought a pound of weed, which was more than I really needed for the job. I really was a completely different person at this point, but the hustler was still in me. I started to sell a little after work to my closest friends and people from the job that called me from home. I couldn't keep weed at my sister's house, so I stashed it all in the trunk of my car. I couldn't keep it in my sister's house, because, for one, she wasn't buying that shit, and on top of that, my parole agent was always threatening to pop up at any moment unannounced.

She told me if she ever showed up, she would be with the police and they would be allowed to search the house for guns or drugs. It might seem like I was taking penitentiary chances again, but in reality, the risk was almost nonexistent at the time. The people in charge at my job pretty much knew what was going on and just looked the other way, and after work it was just family and friends. I didn't consider my little weed hustle that serious but at the time, it was the best decision I could've made for myself to take care of all my responsibilities and still have some money left for myself. I don't regret that decision at all, but soon, what started out as extra money would grow to be more than I'd planned it to be.

THE ALMIGHTY DOLLAR

I'D ALWAYS HEARD ABOUT and witnessed people getting these big income tax checks that they would furnish their whole house with or give it to someone to flip, but since I'd never had a job, I wasn't eligible for any tax money until now. I was happy when the next year came around and I was able to file for the first time. I received a five-thousand-dollar refund that pumped some much-needed finances into my situation at the time. I was able to move out of my sister's house and get my own apartment, which was my proudest moment since I'd been home.

By now, a lot of people knew about me selling weed, and since I had my own place, I didn't have to stash it outside in my car anymore. I never told my parole officer I moved, so I wasn't worried about her showing up. I kept telling myself it was only weed as my clientele grew, and I invested in more pounds. I won't make any excuses for my way of thinking at this point. People just kept seeking me out and I kept supplying them. Like I said, I'm hustler by nature and it's very hard to get a tiger to change his stripes. When I saw an opportunity to better my situation with very little risk, I jumped at the chance.

Before I knew it, I was flipping pounds every week, still mostly through the job. I fronted a lot of it out to other people just to keep from taking any penitentiary chances. It got to a point that I really didn't need the job, but I wasn't going to depend on the hustle as my only income ever again. I knew how you could be up one minute and down the next, and I also knew God was still watching. So, I took my ass to work every

KING BENJAMIN

day whether I needed the money or not. I finally bought a computer and started to focus on my writing again. I knew I wanted to put out my book *Cry Baby* first. It was the book that had been read by other people in jail and had incredible feedback. I knew it was going to be a book that put my name on the map, something different from the average recycled stories. I started to type it up on my computer every day.

While I was doing that, the weed clientele began to spread outside of just coworkers, family, and friends. On the weekends I spent time with my kids, and I'd get with Marie, who I was steadily falling deeper for. Life was good, and I couldn't complain. I took my kids everywhere and bought them whatever they asked for. I went on vacation to Las Vegas and had a ball. The hustle afforded me the freedom I wouldn't have had otherwise at my payrate.

But between working, hustling, spending time with my kids, and having a social life, I wasn't making much progress on my writing or even typing up the first book. I wanted to self-publish, but I looked up a year later and I still wasn't finished even typing up the rough draft. I still held on to my vision and my purpose. I was going to be an author one day. It wasn't that I was lacking focus or getting sidetracked.

My everyday life was filled to the brim with obligations, leaving me no time to work on my passion. I was working eight hours a day and after that, I was now going straight to making drop-offs to all my customers that were waiting for me as soon as I got off work. Sometimes I'd drive around all day selling weed until it was time to come home, eat, shower, and go to sleep. This went on for the last twelve months of my parole. The entire time, I kept telling myself it's only weed, it's only weed. Now weed is legal everywhere, and I look forward to getting back into the game one day. Legally.

The day I got off parole was one of the happiest moments of my entire life. I'd been saying that I wasn't going back to prison, but once I started taking chances that could possibly

FIGHT OF MY LIFE

send me back to prison, there was always that small fear in the back of my mind. I prayed relentlessly that God understood my decisions and saw fit to keep me on the streets. I felt I was doing a lot to make the people I loved lives better, even if I was still cutting some corners. After being out of jail for two years, I actually needed the job and the weed hustle to keep up with the lifestyle I'd created. I always dressed like I was still a drug dealer, and I spoiled Marie even though we weren't in a real relationship.

By now, I'd realized that as much as I loved her, we weren't meant to be a couple. We got along much better as friends, but I still went out of my way to let her know that although I had a lot of women in my life now, she was the one who had my full attention. After I was off parole, I saw another money opportunity at my job that had been there all along. It was kind of the same scenario of supply and demand. Like a lot of jobs, people liked to borrow money until payday, but sometimes there was no one to loan it to them. I started loan sharking to meet the demand that was already there.

There were several loan sharks, but I quickly became the most consistent because I always had extras. Since I was always available, I became the go-to guy. Again, I didn't see this as going back on any promise I'd made to myself. I was off parole, I was still working, and I was still moving towards my goal to be an author. The job was keeping me off the streets, so I knew I would keep working until I no longer needed to. I promised myself when I quit, I would be making legit money off books. In the meantime, I worked my low-paying gig, and I did what I did best. I hustled. I also prayed that God guided me in the direction of my goals for the future. Soon, I started to attend church, just trying to stay as close to God as possible while I figured things out. I would probably show up at least two Sundays out of the month just honestly trying to feel my way through it and maybe find a church home.

The biggest and probably the most important rule in the hustle game is to never shit where you sleep. Around this time,

KING BENJAMIN

I made the mistake of bending that rule a little for the first time in my life. There were about thirty different people in the streets that I supplied weed to on a regular. Out of those thirty, there were two or three people I started letting come to my house because of the relationship we had. They were considered more like family than customers because I'd known them all my life. One of those people was a girl I'd known since she was 12, and she was now in her 30s, that lived only a few minutes away from me.

I considered her family because she was Sal's cousin and Sal was like a brother to me. So when she would want an ounce or something and it was getting late or I didn't feel like coming back outside, I'd let her stop by just as long as she called first. One time she stopped by and her younger brother came with her. I was a little uncomfortable with this from the start, even though I'd known both Tina and Toby their whole lives. Toby was a lot like me when I was younger, in the sense that if he was hurting, there was no telling what he might try and pull. But I knew he knew my reputation, so I figured he wouldn't try me.

As the next few weeks passed, she started to send Toby to my house just because she was too lazy to make the drive herself. I didn't complain, but I still was a little iffy about it in the back of my head. I didn't have any real rationale to tell Toby not to come, so I continued to allow it. Sometimes when I would be running around all day, I'd end up leaving some weed in my car overnight. It was never more than a quarter pound, but if Toby stopped by and I knew I had some weed in the car, I'd go out to the car and get what he wanted.

Once it became a pattern, I realized that he knew I probably left weed in my car all night. Shortly after he made a few trips, my car was broken into and all the weed was stolen. Nothing else, just the weed. Nobody in or around my apartment building knew that I sold weed. Toby was the prime suspect from day one. To make matters worse, nobody from

FIGHT OF MY LIFE

his family called me for anything in the following weeks. Had they called and came through to buy more weed, I would've just written off my theory. Them disappearing had all but confirmed it.

I never felt like the sister was in on it. She was a hustler who made her own money, but Toby was struggling at the time. My guess was he was supplying her with the weed, so she didn't need me. My first thought was an act of violence, but I quickly discarded it. I didn't own a gun and hadn't had to get physical with anybody in years. I told myself it was really just the devil planting seeds in my head. I'd purposely stayed away from guns because I knew eventually something would happen, and if I had one, I was most likely to use it.

So far, I stuck to my rules on not carrying guns, robbing, or selling crack. I never really thought about my moral compass on whooping some ass, but I didn't want to get back in that head space, so I had to figure out another way. I thought about Toby for days to come, and I talked to some people I respected about it. Everyone said the same thing. If I wasn't one hundred percent sure it was him, then I shouldn't move on it. It made sense, but I didn't want to take a loss like that. I felt disrespected. Eventually, I decided to let it slide. For the sake of my future and staying out of trouble for my kids, I had to start thinking like a grown up. As time went by, I even started to sell weed to the sister again, but I never allowed her to come to my house.

Every time I would see Toby, I'd feel played, but there was always something in the back of my mind saying 'what if he really didn't do it?' As more time passed, I began to feel good that I didn't take any action against him. My life was going good, I didn't need for anything, and when the next tax season came around, I got another financial boost. One day, Toby asked me for some weed and so much time had passed, I didn't think anything of it. He only wanted a half ounce, but the weed was so strong I saw shock in his eyes when he smelled it.

KING BENJAMIN

"You got some more of this shit?" he quickly asked.

"Yeah," I replied.

"A lot?" he continued.

I didn't know Toby's financial status at this time, but judging by the fact that he was still living in his sister's basement, I figured hadn't much changed.

"I got enough for whatever you need," I told him.

"Shit, I'ma be at you," he claimed.

I left the house thinking it was strange that he didn't ask me any prices on the weight he was so interested in purchasing. All he asked was did I have a lot of it. It was two nights later when someone broke in my car again and stole some more ounces. I'd drifted into the lazy habit of leaving some in the car again after a lot of long days. I can't explain the type of anger that ran through my body. I was one thousand percent sure that it was Toby now. There was no way to convince me otherwise.

This was a prime example of why I didn't believe in letting shit slide when I was knee deep in the streets. I couldn't let it slide this time. If I let this one go, there was no doubt he'd be waiting for me outside with a ski mask on the next time. I thought my little low-key hustle while I punched the clock would keep me out of trouble and away from the violence that plagued my past.

After the second time, I threw all my peace and serenity talk out of the window. I quickly resorted back to my old ways. I bought a gun the next day and went looking for Toby. Here I was again, about to lay it all on the line because my pride couldn't let it go. I thought I had completely changed, but I had not. I went by Tina's house looking for Toby, but he was nowhere to be found. I went by every other spot I thought he might be, but he was MIA.

FIGHT OF MY LIFE

Not being able to find him was just more confirmation that he was the one behind both break-ins. After about two weeks, I grew tired of looking for him. I still had plans to shoot him on sight, but I couldn't keep riding around with a gun. I hate to admit it, but my temper had gotten the best of me and everything I loved and cared about was put on the back burner while the devil got behind the wheel again. I had to face the facts of who I was. When I felt disrespected, there was no limit to what I would do and what promises I would break. I'd broken another promise and back slid down a dark road again, but luckily, God still wasn't done with me.

From the time I'd started pushing weed, things were going okay for me. I knew it would take some time to accomplish my major goals, but I was progressing slowly. I was a bachelor with a couple women friends in my life that I really cared for and enjoyed being around, plus I was raising my kids the way I planned to. The best part of it all was, I hadn't come in contact with the law at all. I knew this situation with Toby could change that, but I couldn't see a result I could live with without him paying for what he'd done.

I felt like if I let this slide, all the years of work I'd put in to earn my name and respect would've been in vain. I wasn't the most well-known dude in my city by any stretch of the imagination, but the niggas that knew me respected me. That respect still mattered to me. I'd never actually tried to fire the gun I'd got off the streets when I bought it. One day I decided to see if it worked properly so I didn't find myself in a jam, and I came to find out the gun wouldn't even shoot. Someone had sold me a lemon. All this time I'd been riding around with a gun that wouldn't even shoot. There was no way I was about to kill Toby even if I had caught up with him.

I didn't know whether to be mad at myself for not checking the gun or mad at the nigga that sold it to me. I knew this guy pretty good. He wasn't the type to have guns just sitting around that he never intended to use. It didn't take me long to realize the irony of it all as I sat in my apartment that

KING BENJAMIN

night a little in awe. Was God really once again trying to save me from myself? And if so, why? We did He even care at this point? I wondered could he really have a glorious plan for my life like Joyce Meyer said.

I woke up the next day with more questions than answers, but the one thing that continued to taunt me in my sleep was the fact that someone had fucked me over not once, but twice. There was no way I would ever get a good night's sleep knowing I had been played that way. Every day that went by after that, I tried to reason with myself to see if there was some way I could let this go and focus on my future. I was stuck in the mental battlefield with landmines all around me. As bad as I wanted to, I just couldn't leave it alone.

I knew that Toby wasn't soft, so if I ran up on him, I had to be ready for whatever. He might have been broke, but I knew he was with whatever I was with for sure. I also knew that God was trying His best to keep me alive and out of the penitentiary. I never went and tried to replace the gun that didn't work. I realized why it didn't work and I was able to come to grips with the fact that it wasn't meant for me to kill Toby.

Because of our difference in size, I did, however, put a baseball bat in my backseat with intention of leaving him a bloody mess whenever I ran into him. That was my new plan, and once I had a new plan, I could sleep with peace at night. I no longer had to worry about police pulling me over with weed and a gun in the car. Now that I wasn't on parole, the weed wasn't a big deal, but the gun was a five-year bid. The Fourth of July rolled around and I didn't have much planned for the day. I was gonna spend the day at my boy Sal's house drinking and eating up their food.

I remember the day being super busy because everyone always loaded up on weed for the holidays. I spent the early part of my day making drop-offs and by night fall, I was just making it to Sal's house for my first drink. He told me he was

FIGHT OF MY LIFE

about to go over his cousin Tina's house for some drinks. Tina and Sal had always been close throughout the years. Sal knew about my beef with Toby and agreed with me that it was him that had stolen from me. By now everything had died down, so I don't think he thought much into it when he asked me did I want to follow him to Tina's house. I quickly agreed, hoping to run into Toby.

I still hadn't seen him in the months that passed, but today was a holiday. I was almost positive he would be there today. I was anxious to see his face and look in his eyes, knowing he'd been missing for months. When I pulled up and parked across the street from Tina's house, I saw a lot of people outside. A lot of Tina's family and their kids. I knew this wasn't the time to jump out with a baseball bat and get busy.

I'd never even thought things through on the drive over. But as I got out of my car and walked across the street, I quickly spotted Toby sitting in the grass by the side door. My blood began to boil almost immediately. Toby was bigger than me in height and size, plus I'd never heard of him taking a loss in a fist fight. But the closer I got, I knew we had to scrap. There was only one way to settle this that would allow me to sleep at night. Like men. Right here, right now. I knew he didn't know what to expect from me, so I had the element of surprise on my side. There was no telling when I'd see Toby again. I walked straight by everyone else and went right up to Toby.

"Toby, let me holla at you," I said.

He stood up and walked my way. I eased off away from everybody just far enough to make him believe I wanted to have a private conversation. I had to make every swing count because if not, I knew I was in trouble. While his guard was down, I commenced to punching Toby. I hit him four times in the face before he even realized he was in a fight. We locked horns and started trading punches. When I got a free hand, I socked him in the face as hard as I could repeatedly. I was

KING BENJAMIN

faster, but he had a heavy-handed punch. Everyone around was in a panic, running, yelling, and trying to break up the fight. Eventually, Toby gave me one hard shove that sent me stumbling backwards. While I was stumbling, he ran up and caught me with a couple big shots. Because I was surrounded by his family, most of the people trying to break up the fight tried to grab me instead of him, leaving me open for even more blows to the head and face. The fight shifted in his favor quickly. When I finally broke free of all the people trying to break up the fight, I spun around and stepped out into the middle of the street. I was furious because I hadn't been able to defend myself while I was being held by his family. I tore off my shirt and tossed it in the streets, inviting Toby to join me and finish the fight. I could feel my face burning from being hit, but I was more than ready for the second round.

"Let's go, nigga! Let's go!" I shouted, waiting for him to join me in the streets.

My adrenaline was pumping hard. I was ready to see how much either one of us had left. Instead of joining me in the street, Toby rushed to his car and told his girlfriend to get in. He got in the car and drove off as quick as he could. I don't think Toby was afraid to continue the fight at all. I realized now that he probably thought there would be gunplay coming, but as I stood in the middle of the street feeling my eye swelling fast, I really just wanted to finish the fight.

I didn't feel like it was over, but Toby was gone, leaving me in the middle of the street shouting for him to come back and fight me. People will be mad when they read this part, I'm sure. I couldn't tell that story if it didn't happen the way I told it. There were too many people there that witnessed it. Too many people that I'm still associated with to this day. Toby was not only my best friend's cousin, he was also my children's mother's cousin as well. It was hard for things to escalate any further than it went that night. Before that night, no one

FIGHT OF MY LIFE

besides Sal knew about my grievance. Now everyone knew I had a problem with Toby.

If that wasn't enough, Tina drove to my house right after the fight and threatened to call the police on me if anything happened to her brother. I knew she wasn't just talking. She wanted me to know she had every intention of snitching. At that point, I was in a losing battle if things continued. I knew it had to be over. I had to let it go now.

THE BIGGEST MENTAL LOSS

AFTER THE FIGHT WITH TOBY, I was feeling a bit down on myself because the fight left me with a black eye that was almost closed shut. I always knew a fight could go either way, but of all the fights I'd had, I'd never had a fight that left me with visible evidence the next day. I wasn't even upset about the outcome. I gave Toby all I had, and I knew in the end, I'd taken the respect from him that I'd come for. Besides, he left with some bruises as well. When I really sat down and had the time to think about it, he was the one the quit, not me.

It was an outcome I could live with moving forward, but my eye was a different story. I walked around with shades on for a couple weeks because I was too embarrassed to let anyone see it. I was still a gangsta to the people around me no matter how much I'd told everyone I'd changed. I couldn't be seen with a black eye that was swollen shut.

As time went on, my eye healed and things went back to normal. It was really time for me to get my focus and shit or get off the pot with this book thing. During the time since I'd been home, I studied the Law of Attraction continuously and learned to use it to my advantage frequently. I began trying to envision what my book *Cry Baby* would look like when I got a book cover for it, and what it would feel like to be a published author. I started a Facebook page in 2010 just for the purpose of promoting myself as an author. Social media was something

FIGHT OF MY LIFE

I would've never even considered doing if I wasn't chasing a dream, but it would later turn out to mean a lot to me.

As I continued my search into universal laws and my search for truth, I began to lose interest in traditional religion. Each church I tried to attend just didn't feel right for me. I found one that had a pastor from the Eastside that seemed to be down to earth but the more I went, the more I realized that the church was asking for a lot of money each week. There was the regular church tithes and then there was a fund for improvements on the church and then another fund for helping people in need.

I didn't have a problem with where the money was going but to me, it seemed like most of the people in the church were people in need and therefore didn't have the money to contribute to all of it. After a while, I just decided to fall back and develop my own relationship with God to the best of my ability.

At my job, I was still the man to see for anything you needed. I could feel the tension rising between me and some of the people that had been there much longer than I had. The most tension seemed to be coming from the friend of mine that actually got me the job. It seemed that I didn't know Terry as well as I thought I did. He was my supervisor and he never tried to boss me around or anything, but the longer I stayed there the more I prospered financially, and he turned into a real hater. So much so that I'd write about the whole experience years later in a book titled *Wash You off My Skin*.

He was jealous about the girl I was screwing at the time, jealous of the money I was making that was his money before I arrived, and jealous of the fact that we were in the same age bracket and although he was my supervisor, I was beating him in life. It showed in a lot of the petty things he did on a regular as the years went by, but the tension was there from the day I started hustling. I was living a good life, all things considered. Once that clock struck three and we punched out, I was my own boss, making money around the clock, and a lot of guys there just couldn't keep up with me.

Don't get me wrong, I was living a pretty regular life. It wasn't super lavish or anything, but I was doing good, and it showed. I was looking into self-publishing my book and I started telling people for the first time that I was going to be an author. I think the fact that I had a plan to get me out of this dead-end job frustrated the people I worked with even more, especially Terry.

Nobody else wanted out. They were content chasing the young girls around and making scraps to pay bills with. I was learning how to use my mind to get ahead in life, and I was seeing things I wanted manifesting right before my eyes. I was visualizing a lot, learning how to pray properly, and I was learning all about vibrating higher to better your chances. I remember thinking to myself that I had finally figured out some secrets to life. In a way I had, but I still had a long way to go before learning how to get the maximum benefits from the teachings I was learning. I still had no coping skills to deal with my anger or aggression.

I'd finally gotten my book all typed up and had read up enough on publishing that I felt I was ready to jump headfirst into the game. I'd been promoting the book on social media and gaining a small following. I'd gotten my book cover, ordered my bookmarks, and started planning for a book release party. Once I put the order in for my books, I really started to get excited. I was finally about to do it after all this time. It was an amazing feeling and once again, I started to get that adrenaline rush that came with a sense of accomplishment. My lil' ghetto ass was about to become an author. Then, all of sudden, something happened.

After four years at the job, things finally came to a head with me and my supervisor. Things had been brewing between us for a while. We'd argued before but it never escalated. The day it finally boiled over, we got into an altercation about

FIGHT OF MY LIFE

nothing to be honest. It was just time for us to settle things the only way we knew how. Once again, I was going up against someone I had never seen take an L. We went outside in the parking lot across the street and threw hands right there in front of our coworkers. I left the fight without a scratch and so did he, but I can't say I was the victor. It ended with me chasing him back across the street with a car club, still fighting for a win.

Taking an L to Terry in particular was worse than being shot in my eyes, and I could accept it. By this time, it was like we hated each other. It was the biggest mental loss I've ever taken. Even though it was probably at least 18 months a part, I had taken two Ls. I hadn't taken an L since I was in the sixth grade and I was now in my 30s. Being 5'8 around 170 pounds at the time, my hands were something I'd always prided myself on. I had been handing out ass whoopings all my life, no matter what size. I'd stood up to and defeated niggas I was downright afraid to fight as a kid. I no longer had that badge of honor. Now my confidence had been shattered like a fighter past his prime. I was no longer the same when I looked in the mirror.

When I got home that day, the manager of the plant was calling my phone, no doubt to fire me. I never answered the phone because I'd already made up my mind I wasn't going back anyway. There were only two floor supervisors in the whole building, and I'd come to realize I couldn't work under either one. My time at that job was over, and it was time for me to move on with the next chapter of my life. It took me a very long time, but I eventually came to realize that a fair one is just that. You win some, you lose some. You fight enough, you gonna lose. But like we always said in jail, a man ain't never afraid to bleed.

I turned my attention to what I believed I was destined for. I was going to be a successful author, and I wouldn't let anything stand in the way of that. I had to do it now because it was all I had left to believe in. Everything I thought I was had been turned upside down, at least momentarily. I wasn't untouchable, and I wasn't the smartest hustler from my neighborhood. Otherwise, I wouldn't have been where I was in life, and I just had to come to grips with that. I didn't go looking for another job because I had a hustle that could pay my bills for a few months and by then, my book would be out, and I would blow up…or so I thought.

Getting back into the street life was the last thing on my mind. I knew that God had given me a talent and an out, I just had to find a way to manifest my plans into existence. After fighting through my mental battles, I realized how blessed I was to have discovered that my real gift wasn't just my ability to hustle in the streets. I knew a lot of dudes that were stuck in the street hustling because they'd never found another way to survive, and they didn't qualify for any good paying jobs.

Today I believe God gives everyone a way out of the devil's traps, but you have to be actively searching for it and in tune with Him to receive it. The devil, along with today's society, would have a young black man in my position believing he has no choice but to slang dope forever in order to live a decent life. I didn't want to be one of those guys that was 40 years old still ducking and dodging police. It was a sad existence, and I refused to live that life.

People in prison had told me *Cry Baby* was one of the best books they'd ever read. If my test readers were right, I was sitting on a goldmine. I was gonna self-publish and reap all the benefits of my hard work. I'd written the three-hundred-page novel over and over just to get it ready for edits. Now it was finally ready to come to life. At the last minute, a woman named Racheal that helped me out a lot in the beginning told me that I should put out an ebook along with the paperback. Before that conversation, I had no intentions on putting the ebook out because I didn't know anything about it. Little did I know that this was the wave of the future and the paperbacks were quickly becoming a thing of the past.

FIGHT OF MY LIFE

I trusted Racheal's advice and still trust it to this day, so I decided to put out an ebook as well. Hammer and I were still friends, but we didn't see each other as much, just busy with our own individual lives. But I'll never forget the day I found out Hammer was going around telling people that I was never going to release my book. It broke my heart. I had been talking about this book since I'd come home from prison almost five years ago, and I still had no book out.

Hammer was the same friend that allowed me to stay in his apartment when I was on the run. I had a lot of love for him, and I believed in his dreams to pursue a career in music. It fucked me up to realize he didn't believe in me the same way. But the same week I heard about Hammer's not believing in me was the same week that my first book titled *Cry Baby* came out.

It was the best feeling in the world to finally be a published author. It was the first thing I had accomplished since getting my G.E.D that I knew would make my mom extremely proud. The only thing that put a damper on the mood was the fact that I had to cancel my book release party. About a week before my book was set to drop, someone was shot and killed at the lounge, I was set to have the party at.

I knew that even if they opened back up in time, that was gonna scare a lot of people off, and I couldn't afford to pay for another spot on short notice. But I was still on cloud nine, especially when I went to pick up the physical copies and got to hold the book in my hand. Everyone was proud of me and offering me a lot of encouragement. It was a much-needed pick me up after everything that had happened in the previous months. I ordered two hundred copies of my book, which put a big dent in the money I had.

Since I didn't have the release party, I went to work selling my books in the streets. After I hit up all my family and friends, my sales slowed down, but I kept at it. I hit up all the barbershops and salons from east to west. I put my book at all

KING BENJAMIN

the bookstands in the area and any local bookstores I could find to shelve it. I hit downtown with a duffle bag full of books and got my grind on. I mean, I was really going hard pushing *Cry Baby*. But when I looked up, three weeks had passed, and I still had 80 books left. After that, I realized that the ebook, which I priced at seven dollars, wasn't doing that good either.

I kept pushing, but it wasn't long before I realized that I wasn't going to be an overnight success. The problem was, I was spending so much time on the book grind I wasn't making the money I would've usually made pushing weed to pay my bills. After the adrenaline rush was over, and after my high hopes were deflated, I looked up and I was stuck with books that weren't selling and bills to pay. My first check from Amazon was under $100. I went back to my old job and sold about five copies of my book. All I could think about was all I'd given up when I decided to fight my supervisor.

That bullshit job offered me structure and months later, I was just out here struggling with bills and on the verge of desperation again. I didn't sit around feeling sorry for myself, but it was a huge blow to my ego. I had failed as an author. Everybody loved the book. I mean, really, really loved it, but it wasn't selling enough to help me out financially. I had a choice to make. I could go back to the streets, go look for a job, or push forward with my writing career. By now, I had changed so much I knew I wasn't going back to the street life, but I had to do something. I saw Terry that day I went back to my job and I had to just eat the L all over again, but it was important for me to walk in and show my face as a published author.

THE REAL FIGHT BEGINS

THERE'S A POWER WITHIN ALL of us that I'd had only slight brushes with when I first tried moving my life in a different direction. I was aware of it, but I didn't have the time or the know how to study this power and apply it correctly. Years would pass before I became truly awakened to the magnitude of it and realize that God could not do for me what He was trying to do through me.

When I first decided to become an author, I gave myself five years to become successful. I told myself if I wasn't successful in five years, then I had my permission to do whatever I wanted to do with my life at that point, because I would've given it everything I had. After the initial shock wore off that I wasn't going to be an overnight success, I went to work preparing my second project for release while trying to figure out what went wrong the first time, so it didn't happen again. I was still pushing *Cry Baby* on the internet and selling physical copies whenever I could, but the money wasn't adding up to much.

I held on to my vision, and I continued to gain support because the book was so different than anything else that was out at the time. This was around the time I met a woman that would become one of my best friends and a very significant piece of the puzzle that was my future. Lakelia Deloach-Lucas aka Author Blackbyrd found me on Facebook and purchased my debut novel as we were trading information about the publishing process. After reading it, she loved the book so much she began to tell people about it. She was also in the process of releasing her first book, which was a non-fiction title called *Get Over Him Girl*.

We started to talk about book stuff on a regular and I would give her whatever pointers I had on self-publishing. Somehow, we just clicked, and we started to help one another out all we could. She would gift all of her friends and family my ebook, and I would tell people I knew about her upcoming title. I spent most of my days typing up my second novel titled *Gank Masterz*. This was to be my first series, and I still had two more parts to write, so I started writing the sequel while I was typing up the first book. I was doing whatever I could do to pay bills, but not taking any chances that would land me back in prison. I still hustled a little weed and I even started selling car insurance.

I knew if I got caught up doing either one of those things, it wouldn't send me back to prison and totally derail me and my plans. Right before I was ready to release my second novel, I met India Norfleet-Lewis and Danielle Marcus, who were also new authors trying to find their way through the self-publishing maze. I introduced the two of them to Lakelia and we all went out to dinner one day. I remember it being one of those moments that I knew I was right where I was supposed to be. Sitting at the table with a bunch of writers, I felt so at home. When we began to discuss our ideas, our struggles, and our concerns, a bond and an unspoken alliance was formed. Never in my life had I ever just naturally meshed with people the way I did with these authors that I only had one real thing in common with, which was books. Our lives and circumstances were completely different, yet we meshed so well.

Soon, we came up with a name for a little circle, and we called ourselves the Detroit Authors Alliance. Our only goal from the start was to help one another any way we could and share information and resources. Together, we found our way through the maze and were there to support one another on

FIGHT OF MY LIFE

anything book related. A whole year passed before I was able to self-publish my second novel. The good thing about that was by now, a lot of people had read *Cry Baby* and were anticipating a new release from me. I had a lot more knowledge of the book business and a lot more contacts. My plan was to hit the road this time and do some book signings state to state to really get my name out there.

In December of 2013, I dropped my second novel, *Gank Masterz*. I spent every dime I could come up with on promotion and marketing. I was branding myself and the DAA movement that we'd started. I got T-shirts printed, I did a book trailer, ordered bookmarks, and paid people to promote on the internet. The book started off much better than my first release. There was even a little hype around it, so I pumped it as hard as I could. My DAA team helped me pump it as well.

I got in touch with a publicist from Philly and set up two book signing events in her city. I was feeling like I was on my way to living my dreams. I went out to dinner with my author crew, feeling like it was a celebratory event. My second book was out, and things were going good. We had a great time and a lot of laughs. I went home that night just thinking about the bond we had created and how our friendships were all continuing to grow collectively and individually. The next morning, I woke up and my car was gone. Someone had stolen it out of my driveway. I was devastated. It was the worst timing in the world because I had just dumped all my money off into putting the book out. I called and reported it stolen, but I knew I'd never see my car again in one piece.

The next few days, I sat around like a wounded dog trying to figure out how to bounce back from this. I didn't know it then, but this event had totally changed my whole vibration, which in turn influenced the other areas of my life as well. I was no longer excited about my new book and soon, it started to lose momentum in sales. There wasn't much I could do to pick it back up either. I'd already spent all I could on promotion and now I had a much bigger problem to deal with.

KING BENJAMIN

With no car, I had no hustle. With no hustle, I couldn't pay my bills. I had to cancel the book signings I had set up and hold off on everything book related. I'd sold enough to know I would make a lot more off my second book than I did the first one, so I didn't feel like a complete failure, but I was a long way from the success I dreamed of.

****

It took me some time, but I hustled up on another car. Wasn't the car I wanted, but I was glad to be back on the road. By that time, I was so behind on bills I needed guaranteed money, and I needed it fast. I decided it was time to go back to work, so I went to a few temp services, knowing that was the fastest way to get a paycheck. I landed at a job called Budco that a lot of people from my area had worked at or were familiar with. It was one of those jobs that was easy to get, and people came and left constantly because the job was way too demanding for such shitty pay.

I didn't know all of this going in, but I learned about it fast. I didn't care what the pay was, I was just trying to keep from getting evicted. I continued to visualize my success as an author in as much detail as possible. As time went on, I came to enjoy being back in the grind of the plant life. There were a lot of women to flirt with and keep you company, which for men was the biggest asset a minimum wage job could offer. I began to apply an attitude of gratitude to my everyday life, just being thankful for all the small things. I'd told myself in prison that I would always be grateful from my freedom, my family, and my health. I still had all three.

Slowly, I was able to catch up on my bills, but there was no way I could afford to put a book out. Meantime, my readers were getting antsy and coming in my inbox asking for part two

FIGHT OF MY LIFE

of *Gank Masterz*. This was the first time I ever actually thought about signing with a publishing company. There were a couple of independent companies on the rise at the time, and one of my closest author friends had signed with one and was making a lot of money. It sounded like the easy solution to my problem but the more I learned, I didn't think it was.

I quickly realized that most of the independent publishing companies that were emerging on the scene were really just opportunistic hustlers who were corrupting, devaluing, and making a mockery of the urban literary community. The 0.99 cent book had taken over, and there were all kinds of behind-the-scenes scams going on to manipulate Amazon's system. On top of that, a lot of these publishers weren't allowing the authors much creative control. They'd take a book and change the title to the most ridiculous thing they could think of. Then they just flat out started telling the authors what to write about.

I didn't want any parts of it. I had to do this my way, so I kept grinding and kept writing whenever I could find the time. It was hard watching from the sidelines as authors realized their dreams and became overnight successes with trickery and scams. They were living my dream. Everyone knew their names and then some went on to establish their own independent publishing companies. Some authors couldn't take it and began smear campaigns, bashing the companies and their authors, but I never hated or bashed anyone. I stayed focused on my goals and prayed for guidance. While all of this was happening, I was also still on a journey of self-discovery and spirituality.

This was around the time I was introduced to one of the greatest books I've ever read called *Think and Grow Rich* by Napoleon Hill. I'd heard so many successful people talk about how that book had changed their life and once I read it, I knew one day I would be one of them. The book just made so much sense to me, but it wasn't the kind of book that you could just read and go on with your life, which was basically what I did at first. I had such a burning desire to take on the world after

KING BENJAMIN

reading it, I jumped back into the author world head first, just determined to make it somehow. I started promoting myself again heavy as I closed in on finishing up *Gank Masterz 2*. I scrambled up on enough money to get it edited and put it out. I was so relieved to be back doing what I loved, but the euphoria was short lived. Whatever money I spent on putting part 2 out was probably what I made off of the book.

Okay, cool. This is all a part of paying dues, I said. This is the price you pay for staying independent and writing what you want to write, I told myself. Tax time rolled around, and I had the financial boost that tax time brings to help me put out another book. Instead of trying to put out the finale to the *Gank Masterz* series, I decided to put out the first book I'd ever written since it was already finished. I spent all the extra money I could on promotions and marketing. This book had more of a love story spin with a street element than a straight street lit title.

My fourth title had more success than anything I'd published in the past, and it gave me some much-needed confidence. It wasn't a homerun, but it was a hit. This was around the time of the introduction of Kindle Unlimited, which was a program Amazon used as the new pay system for authors. Kindle Unlimited meant that readers could now read as many books as they wanted for $10 a month, and authors would get paid by pages read from the books. It was definitely a better system for me than the one before that where new authors had to sell thousands of 0.99 cent books in order to make any money.

I went to work on the sequel to *The War Report*, but I took my time. I wanted readers to know that my skills were improving with each new release, so I refused to rush it. Meanwhile, others were putting out straight garbage and making a killing off of a bunch of curse words and over-the-top drama. A lot of the books weren't even edited. It was a sign of the times. Six months later, when I put out the sequel to *The*

FIGHT OF MY LIFE

War Report, the buzz had died and people were no longer interested. All the hot titles had the word "Bitch" in it. It seemed like I couldn't win by playing fair and just trying to be a serious writer and respecting my craft. So, I went back to my dead-end job, dazed and confused. It's right here that I have to make a point. I was never focused on finding a better job, no matter what type of struggles I went through.

Maybe I should've looked for something better, but as long as my daughter had what she needed, I was focused on one thing, and that was becoming a fulltime author. I wasn't raising my stepson any longer. When he turned 12, he decided he didn't really want the relationship anymore. He stopped coming to my house with my daughter and his mom stopped trying to help me keep the bond. It was a hurtful experience but if neither of them wanted to keep us close, there was nothing I could do but move on. This is another one of those things I won't go into more detail about, for obvious reasons. I initially wrote an entire chapter about our disconnect but later deleted it. Some things need to remain private.

Each time I put out a book, I was always thinking it would be the one to catapult me to unthinkable heights. I knew that people loved my work, but what I didn't know was all the behind the scenes things people were doing to push past all the competition and hit that bestsellers list. One day I was having a conversation with a very successful author, whose pen game I respected, via inbox. I was just honestly searching for answers on how to get my name out and more exposure for my brand.

She told me she was actually planning to start her own company and publish authors and that if I was interested, she would was give me a fifty/fifty split of the royalties. By now, I was really growing frustrated with the rollercoaster that never went too high for too long. I tried it my way and it just wasn't working. After talking it over with my author friends, I decided that this was probably the best move for me. If nothing else came from it, I knew she could give me the exposure I desperately needed.

KING BENJAMIN

We agreed I'd signed a one-book deal and see how things went. If we were both happy, we would move on from there. With the author having more education and a stronger background in writing, I immediately learned some things from her. Most of what she did to the book, I will admit, made it better. I was thinking this was really a relationship that could work. This author had such a strong name, I knew that if we promoted the book properly that there would be no turning back. Sadly, the exact opposite happened.

I didn't have any money to spend on promotion, which was one of the reasons I decided to take the deal. The person who had plenty of money to spend on promotions didn't spend a dime. When the book dropped, it debuted on the charts ranked at 1000 in the world. That means out of the millions of books on Amazon, there's only 999 other books selling better than yours. Then after that, it went to 750 and then 730. This number is different than the actual bestsellers number. This number tells you how many books you sold each hour. This was by far the best performance I'd ever had for a new release, and it was strictly based on her name and the small fan base I'd built. But after the first day, she never promoted the book again in any shape, form, or fashion.

I couldn't believe it. Slowly, the book just dropped in rankings day after day, and there was nothing I could do or nothing she wanted to do. Then when the royalties came, which was only about a thousand dollars, she tried to keep the majority of it, claiming she had to recoup the money she'd spent publishing the book. What money? I knew she hadn't spent any besides maybe a hundred on the book cover and a couple hundred on her cousin to edit. I found a bunch of errors even after getting the book back from her editor, so I knew she hadn't paid much. As many mistakes as I found in the book when she sent it back to me, I can honestly say the editing couldn't have been more than that. So she was basically trying to fuck me out of the little money I did make off the book.

FIGHT OF MY LIFE

I won't get off into any more detail of how that ended, but let's just say that was my one and only attempt at handing over my work and trusting it with someone else. After that, I was completely lost. If I had any confidence in my future as an author, it was going to take some time to build it back up. I still had my vision, and I still believed it would happen, I just had no idea of when and how. And this is why my book had to be called the *Fight of My Life*. There's no other way to describe everything that I went through before things finally turned around for me. It was a dog fight to the end.

After my experience with a publisher, I got fed up. The overnight success of others was starting to get the best of me. All I needed was one good book to really get noticed and turn my life around, but true success evaded me still. I saw people spending literally no money putting a book out and making thousands, and here I was, had spent thousands and wasn't making a dime. I'd robbed Peter to pay Paul and spent bill money just to put out a book and promote it properly. Before I left Budco, I'd even go so far as to use my rent money to put out books, because that's how much I believed that this was meant to be. I went all in and it cost me everything, because I just knew that I couldn't live the nine-to-five life for the rest of my life, and I couldn't go back to the streets. I never wanted anything so badly that was so hard to obtain.

In 2014, I'd been out of jail for seven years and I was barely getting by. Then the job I had laid everyone off, and I wasn't even getting by. Out of pure desperation, I started trying to edit my own books and put them out just because I needed some money. I figured this was better than grabbing a gun or kicking in someone's door. The worst thing that could happen is I hinder my already stalling career, but the best that could happen was that I could blow up like so many I'd seen do already off of books that weren't edited properly or weren't good at all. Then I could go back to doing things the right way.

None of it worked out for me at the time the way that I wanted. I dropped flop after flop of some of the best books

KING BENJAMIN

I've ever written, basically due to lack of proper promotion more than my bad editing. I was still happy to have a check from Amazon at the end of the month no matter what it was. During this time, I did whatever I could think of to legally make money. No matter what, I still had a daughter to raise and provide for. I shoveled snow at Comerica Park and did whatever other jobs a temp service offered me. I remember coming home and drinking until I passed out because I hated my life. I was stuck on a treadmill going nowhere.

Eventually, the money coming in just didn't add up to what was needed to pay the bills and I was given an eviction notice. I stalled them out by taking them to court and by the time the courts were actually ready to evict me, tax season hit, and I was able to move into another place without having my things tossed on the curb. Every year, tax season would give me a lifeline, but I knew that I just couldn't go on this way. The money I was getting in February was the money I was expecting to get every month from books.

When I moved into my new place, I decided I needed to revisit this *Think and Grow Rich* strategy. I was always at peace whenever I was studying any type of self-improvement material, but especially that one. Every time I went back to it, I seemed to get some new insight on my best next moves. It still didn't happen overnight, but once I started to work on myself again, the seeds I planted from years ago would finally start to bloom.

DREAM CHASER

AFTER LISTENING TO *Think and Grow Rich* on audiobook, I ran around into a seminar on YouTube titled *Born Rich* by Bob Procter. If *Think and Grow Rich* was the spark I needed, *Born Rich* was the flame. A ten-hour seminar on exactly how the mind works in accordance with goals, vibration, and the Law of Attraction. Because it was more current and detailed than Napoleon Hill's book, it was able to fill in all the missing gaps that I really needed to expand my thinking. As Bob went over the material, each hour was like unlocking a new and untapped level of thinking as well as coping skills for me. I realized the importance of relaxation and meditation.

I learned how my level of expectation had been severely compromised by the failures I'd suffered. I also learned how to turn it all around quickly. This shit really lit a fire under my ass. I started studying the *Born Rich* seminars in all my free time. I knew right then the answers were coming soon, I just needed to get my focus on the goal again. There's no better feeling in the world of when you reach that highest level of expectation and faith. No matter what's going on in your life, you just know you are about to manifest some shit!

One thing I had come to realize over the past year was that the only difference between my books and a lot of other bestsellers' books was that there was a female author behind the pen, and most of them had a crazy title that caught attention. Woman loved to read female authors. They loved connecting with them on social media to see how relatable they were as well as getting all up in their business. I can only assume they wanted to know the author to find out if they were the type of person they respected, related to, or even admired. That's when it hit me that I needed to create another pen name. A catchy female pen name that would make people flock to the books and see what she had to say.

I wouldn't make a fake page for her and all that like some had done in the past, but that was a good thing because this way, there was no one to look up, no one to connect with, and no one to judge. You either liked her books strictly based on skillset, or you didn't. The crazy part was, I had just done a short story challenge a couple months before where I wrote the craziest shit I could think off just to draw attention from the readers.

They ate it up so much that I decided to keep the story and vowed to finish it. That short story would later become one of the books I wrote under my female pen name Karizma Keys. But first, I needed to connect her name to me in some way so people would have some incentive to read this new author that nobody had ever heard of, other than the fact that she was a female. As it turned out, writing books under my second pen name was the best decision I've ever made probably still to this day.

I had to make a decision on what was most important at the time. Was it the craft or my ability to hustle? As always, the hustle won. I was at the end of my rope with trying to find solutions to expand my reader base going solely off the fact that I was dope and original. I conjured up one of the most fast-paced, over-the-top stories I could think of. I titled it *We Out Here* and put two names on the cover, King Benjamin and Karizma Keys.

I put her name first, even though nobody had ever heard of her. I needed people to see that female name on the cover. By now, I had learned how to get the maximum benefits out of free days on Amazon, so I didn't even try and sell it to my

FIGHT OF MY LIFE

fans. I knew it wasn't edited properly so I didn't want the negative feedback from them if they paid for it. I published it and gave it away for free. I wasn't trying to gain their support, I already had it. I was trying to gain the support of people that never heard of me or her. The people that seemed to eat up anything wild and ridiculous. I put the book out and I woke up every day with setting my intentions for success.

It worked like a charm. After the free days were over, the book started selling like crazy. Then I dropped part two and three and those books continued to sell, keeping the series up in the top rankings. I made more money than I'd ever made in all my years as an author off that first series. Part one gave me my first number one bestseller as well. The feeling was so amazing, I was on a natural high for weeks. I was so glad I didn't give up like I wanted to. It was a defining moment, and I always think about that period in my life every time I hear the clip of Nipsey Hussle's interview where he talked about going through every emotion but not giving up. It was the story of my life.

After going number one with Karizma Keys, I knew that it was confirmation that I needed to stay in the game and keep writing. But I had to go with the hot hand. I couldn't go back to what wasn't working, so I quickly began to come up with another Karizma Keys title, but this wouldn't have my name on it at all. I'd noticed that just about any book with the words "savage" and "bitch" in the title were selling at the moment. It wasn't the type of title that King Benjamin would write, but it was definitely something Karizma Keys would. I had to treat the game like I was hustling in the streets if I was going to keep making good money. That's around the time I stumbled across the story I'd written in the short story challenge, and I realized it was exactly what I was looking for. I finished the story and put it out with the title *Savages and Side Bitches*.

Just like the last time, the book took off immediately. I didn't even put it out until I had written two books to the series already, so I was able to follow right up with the sequel. By the time the second one dropped, the first one had become a number one bestseller. It was amazing how a female name and crazy title could change everything. Just a simple adjustment changed the course of my life completely. I wrote four books to the series and by the time I put out the last book, I was getting checks over five thousand dollars every month.

When things really started to take off, I was at the end of my rope with my job and I was already past my five-year goal I'd set to accomplish success. It all started to fall in place after I made the decision not to give up no matter how long it took. I quit my job as soon as I got the first big check. I was finally living my dream of being a fulltime author. The way it happened was nothing like what I had envisioned when I started out, but I'd done it. I'd proven to myself that my skillset was enough to make it.

Now the only problem was, I still didn't have a big fan base for King Benjamin. While Karizma Keys was growing, King Benjamin was kind of at a standstill. I released a standalone called *Broke and Lonely* that I had put my all into and I knew was an amazing book. It didn't sell nearly as much as Karizma Keys' books, but it brought attention back to me as an author. I realized I had so many books out that as long as I continued to self-publish, I would make money because one book would sell the others.

Even if I only made $1500 off of King Benjamin books, I would make another $3500 to $4500 from Karizma Keys, and I didn't have to split the money with another author because we were one and the same. The hustler in me could live with that. I can't explain the feeling of a dream that you worked so hard for being realized. Being an author had taken me so far away from the streets that I couldn't go back if I wanted to because I wasn't that guy anymore. I was a writer and more importantly, a father. All I had to do now was raise the profile on King Benjamin as a writer and a brand once and for all. I

FIGHT OF MY LIFE

knew I had the skills. My sales and feedback were showing it. I just needed that one big book.

It didn't take long for my common sense to kick in. The books I'd been writing under Karizma Keys were drama filled, fast paced, and action packed. But more importantly, the title and the author's name sold the books, in my opinion. Well, I couldn't change my main pen name since I'd worked too hard to establish it, but I could give my next King Benjamin book a standout title that screamed drama to catch readers' attention. I decided to republish a title that had already been previously published, under a different name. That title and book would become my first number one bestseller as King Benjamin. It was a series called *Lies and Fuckery*. That title sold more books and stayed in the top rankings longer than any King Benjamin book I'd ever published.

It was a great story and those are still some of my favorite characters to this day. I was just glad I'd finally created something in my original pen name that was able to really grab readers' attention. It was a three-part series, so it continued to sell as the next book was released. After the books slowed down, I put the series in a boxset and it shot up the charts all over again. It was hard not to fall in love with the characters that were literally changing my situation. My box sets were actually more profitable than my initial series. After the three-part series was over, the characters were still talking to me, so I started working on a spin-off series.

With the money I made from both bestselling series, I was able to pay for proper editing and reposition myself financially to start enjoying my life. For the first time since being an author, I was able to travel for pleasure, shop freely without worrying about the price tag, and go to the car lot and get what I wanted. I cleaned up my credit and paid off all my traffic tickets plus my back child support. I was finally catching up with myself, catching up with my age. It had been such a long road I couldn't help but wake up in a state of constant gratitude. I knew as an author and entrepreneur that I wasn't

KING BENJAMIN

guaranteed anything, so I stayed on my grind, but I also made the second best decision I'd ever made in my life. I started to learn as much as I could about investing in the stock market. Remember, this was something I always wanted to do since my first time going to prison.

I took me almost twenty years, but it's funny how things that are meant for you always come back around. After doing my own research on how to invest, I opened a brokerage account and started investing. Within a month, I could see the potential of the stock market and how it was synonymous with growing wealth. I won straight out of the gate, but like any new and overemotional investor, I took a loss or two before I learned I needed to come up with an investment strategy.

Once I devised a strategy that fit my style of investing, I never looked back. I continued to invest and learn the game. I saw my money growing instead of just sitting in the bank, and it gave me a thrill like I was flipping coke again. I bought paid courses on how to invest and learned from the people that knew way more than I did. Now I had a second stream of income. Next, I went to work finding a narrator to produce my audio books. Once I began to publish audiobooks, this gave me a third stream of income.

I was finally in a state of flow and being the person I'd seen myself as all those years. I often ask myself, what the hell took me so long? Some people say things don't happen on your time but in God's time. I'll probably never be completely confident I know that answer but if I had to guess, I would say a few things that I know for sure contributed. Karma is very real but more importantly, you can't let the idea of it consume you. You can't let your past dictate your present.

Subconsciously, I was scared of the success I dreamed of because of karma. I was afraid when I reached my peak I'd be tragically killed by my karma. My past trauma had mentally scarred me to the point I had a hard time believing I was worthy of the success I wanted so badly. But this fear wasn't

FIGHT OF MY LIFE

on the surface where I or anyone else could really see it. It was deeply buried in an old and stubborn paradigm.

Lastly, I know now it's important to align with what's meant for you. You know when you're aligned with your divine plan because you won't have to work nearly as hard to accomplish your goal. Once I aligned and blocked out all negativity, things just started to happen. But even when you are perfectly aligned, and everything is going great, you still have to be aware of your old habits and paradigms. They are dream killers.

PARADIGMS DIE HARD

DURING ALL MY YEARS OF self-help study, I read a lot of books and listened to a lot of motivational speakers. It all kept me inspired when I wanted to quit or felt like I was losing faith. Another one of the best books I ever came across was by the late Maxwell Maltz called *Psycho-Cybernetics*. I listened to the audiobook probably two dozen times. In the book, he explains that no matter how hard you try, you can never outperform your true self-image. In every self-help book I read the same thing that was said a different way. The results you get will always be in some way related to the person you truly believe yourself to be, not who you would like to be. That voice in your head that's talking and nobody else can hear. That's the person that controls your life no matter how hard you try to change it.

Maxwell Maltz said the only way to accomplish destroying a bad self-image is to create a new one. When I heard this, it hit me like a brick. I knew that deep down inside, I never felt like I deserved what I wanted, mostly because of my past. Even when I looked at people who I knew had probably done more dirt than me and were successful, I couldn't shake that inner demon I'd been subconsciously fighting without knowing.

Bob Proctor had taught me about paradigm shifts and how to create them, but it was that going back and taking a long, hard look at my original self-image that allowed me to make lasting changes. Bob said that there's something inside of you called a terror barrier. It's that feeling you get when

FIGHT OF MY LIFE

you're so close to reaching goals that you all of a sudden fear the worst going wrong and a lot of times, it does. All hell can break loose right before the finish line and you never know why. It's the terror barrier and the old paradigm fighting to keep you in a stagnated place. Now when you mixed this powerful paradigm with the trauma of street life and poverty, it can feel completely impossible to manifest anything substantial. There's this sense of uncertainty that comes with the next level of your life, and the terror barrier would much rather keep you comfortable in that level of life you're used to than to reach for new heights.

Creating a new self-image for myself allowed me to break through those terror barriers and become that man I always envisioned myself to be. I learned how to fight off panic when something goes wrong before it has a chance to grow stronger. I learned how to expect the best possible outcome even when things are extremely bleak. That stuff is powerful, and more importantly, it actually works! Was it easy? Absolutely not. It took years of reprogramming, meditation, prayer, and sacrifices, but in the end, I can honestly say now that I'm living with purpose.

My life is not perfect by a long shot. I had my last physical altercation back in 2016 when I was trying to break up a brawl with my young dogs and somehow, I got sucker punched. I had to dust the young bull off just to let him and myself know that I still had hands. It made me realize that even in my most peaceful state, I would always have to stay ready for whatever life might bring to my doorstep. I'll always be a man first. I'll always be a little hood, but not everybody from the hood gets to say that they are living their dream. Now I'm creating new goals and I have no doubt in my mind that I will accomplish them. I also want to help as many people from the streets as I can along the way. That would give me the biggest thrill of all, to help someone avoid falling victim to the trap that is the ghetto. To help someone else make a transition from the belly of the beast to living their dreams. I dream big so I know I

KING BENJAMIN

have a long way to go, but at least now I can travel that road with a peace of mind and the freedom of independence that I so desperately longed for all those years.

THE BEST VERSION OF ME

THROUGHOUT MY LIFE, there has always been this distant but constant voice in my head telling me to pipe down. Telling me to be overly cautious about everything. How much I reveal about myself to people, how many chances I take, and how bold to be in the face of adversity. When I was younger, this voice was really strong and as I was facing trials, it only grew stronger. What I learned later in life was that this voice was really my lower self-holding me back from becoming a better version of me.

I know now that I have control over the narrative of my own life. We all have control over the narrative of our own lives. I know it's hard to believe when you've been hit with so many knockout punches and bad hands, but the reality is, we're still standing. That means you can always turn it around. It's literally never too late, but what you must know is that you can never outrun yourself. Your real opinion of yourself will always playout in your circumstances. Like James Allen says in his classic book *As a Man Thinketh*, a man does not get what he hopes and wishes for but what he is.

I don't know if the negative voice ever completely goes away, but I do know that you can shrink it so small that it never has any real effect on your life. The power is in your own self talk. Meditation and affirmations are great tools to use when reprogramming your mind to a new conditioning, but in my

KING BENJAMIN

opinion, nothing is more powerful than thoughts you create, the faith you have in yourself, and the faith you have in that driving force outside of yourself. And to quote another classic title, *The Science of Getting Rich* by Wallace D. Wattles, when in doubt, increase your faith and gratitude. Gratitude truly does keep your mind on the right path and keep you closer to God.

I became the best version of myself when I stopped waiting for my life to be perfect to start living and pursuing my dreams. When I learned to value the present moment, starting right where I was, and trust that God was leading me toward the path to greatness, my life changed for the better. One last thing I have to make clear to everyone that picked up this book in hopes of finding something that would put them on a different and better path. Life is a beautiful experience with a lot of different elements of that beauty. Focusing on longevity as well as your ambitions will lead to a more fulfilling life. Everyone doesn't have to be rich by twenty-five, especially if you have to risk being dead at twenty-six to get there. Life is a marathon.

There's so many amazing things to digest in the later years that a lot of street hustlers will never get to see because they died in their twenties. There's no guarantees in life, but the worst thing is to survive the streets and end up an old dude with no money, no direction, and no skillset. Imagine what the best version of yourself would really look like and start moving towards that version today.

Learn how to love your people that are not blood related. We can never be the best version of ourselves until we learn not to hate our own. We see each other as the enemy so much growing up in the hood because it's usually not the white man who broke in your house or stole your car. It's usually not the white man that set your cousin up to get killed or that hated on you when you finally came up from the trenches. Still, we can't allow those that have succumbed to their lower self to allow us to accept the crab-in-the-bucket mentality. Always remember,

FIGHT OF MY LIFE

there are millions of people that look like you that want you to succeed. I've had more strangers than friends rooting for me my entire career.

Sometimes we just need exposure to a different scene and/or a different group of people. While reading this book, you've been exposed to some of my deepest, darkest secrets, my worst moments, and my biggest triumphs. You've gotten a bird's eye view of the countless times I've recklessly put my life and freedom on the line, only to have God step in and save me from myself. So this book had to be written to show others that it's never too late and that no matter how many times you fail at something, keep fighting. It's your life, and if you care about it, you better fight like hell to make something of it.

Check out the best of King Benjamin Books

Cry Baby 1 & 2
Gank Masterz (A 3 part series)
The War Report (A three part series)
Record Label Romance 1&2
Broke and Lonely
More than I can bare
Roxanne: From Addict to hustler
Wash you off my skin: a forbidden love story
A boss and A thug

Subscribe to www.kingbenjaminpresents.com for updates on book signings, giveaways, and new releases.
Connect on Social Media
Facebook: King's Castle Reading Group
Facebook: Author King Benjamin
Instagram: @AuthorKingBenjamin